NATIONS OF THE WORLD

CHINA

Catherine Field

RAINTREE
STECK-VAUGHN
PUBLISHERS

A Harcourt Company

Austin · New York
www.steck-vaughn.com

Steck-Vaughn Company

First published 2000 by Raintree Steck-Vaughn Publishers,
an imprint of Steck-Vaughn Company.
Copyright © 2000 Brown Partworks Limited.

Library of Congress Cataloging-in-Publication Data

Field, Catherine
   China / Catherine Field
      p.   cm. — (Nations of the world).
   Includes bibliographical references and index.
   Summary: Examines the land, people, and history of China and discusses
its current state of affairs and place in the world today.
   ISBN 0-8172-5781-0
   1. China--Juvenile literature. [1. China] I. Title.
II. Series: Nations of the World (Austin, Tex.)
DS706.F53 2000
951 21--dc21

                                                            99–042579
                                                                 CIP

Printed and bound in the United States
1 2 3 4 5 6 7 8 9 0   04 03 02 01 00 99

Brown Partworks Limited
Project Editor: Robert Anderson
Designer: Joan Curtis
Cartographers: Joan Curtis and William LeBihan
Picture Researcher: Brenda Clynch
Editorial Assistant: Roland Ellis
Index: Kay Ollerenshaw

Raintree Steck-Vaughn
Publishing Director: Walter Kossmann
Project Manager: Joyce Spicer
Editor: Shirley Shalit

Front cover: karst landscape in Guangxi province (background); painting of Confucius (center); Ming porcelain bowl (top left)
Title page: cherry trees in blossom

The acknowledgments on p. 128 form part of this copyright page.

Contents

Foreword

Since ancient times people have gathered together in communities where they could share and trade resources and strive to build a safe and happy environment. Gradually, as populations grew and societies became more complex, communities expanded to become nations—groups of people who felt sufficiently bound by a common heritage to work together for a shared future.

Land has usually played an important role in defining a nation. People have a natural affection for the landscape in which they grew up. They are proud of its natural beauties—the mountains, rivers, and forests—and of the towns and cities that flourish there. People are proud, too, of their nation's history—the shared struggles and achievements that have shaped the way they live today.

Religion, culture, race, and lifestyle, too, have sometimes played a role in fostering a nation's identity. Often, though, a nation includes people of different races, beliefs, and customs. Many have come from distant countries, and some want to preserve their traditional lifestyles.

Nations have rarely been fixed, unchanging things, either territorially or racially. Throughout history, borders have altered, often under the pressure of war, and people have migrated across the globe in search of a new life or of new land or because they are fleeing from oppression or disaster. The world's nations are still changing today: Some nations are breaking up and new nations are forming.

China is one of the world's oldest and largest nations. The cities and towns that grew up in the river valleys of the Chang and Huang stand alongside those of the ancient Middle East and Egypt as the birthplaces of human civilization. China's rulers—both its emperors and, in the 20th century, its communist dictators—have gradually expanded the country to cover much of eastern and central Asia and its peoples. The relationship between the Chinese government and the country's non-Chinese people has not always been happy. The Tibetan people are still fighting for independence and their own right to nationhood.

Introduction

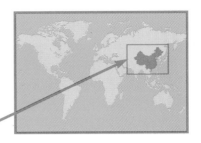

CHINA

China is one of the world's greatest nations. It is the third-largest country in the world after the Russian Federation and Canada and is the largest nation in Asia. At 1.2 billion the population of China is bigger than that of any other country on Earth—about one in every five people on the planet lives in China.

Nevertheless, China remains little known and poorly understood in the West. Few foreigners learn its beautiful but difficult language, and students rarely study its ancient history. Most Westerners' contact with Chinese culture is limited to a trip to their local Chinatown, for example, during the lively New Year celebrations. To many people, China seems as remote and mysterious as it did in the 13th century when Venetian traveler Marco Polo (1254–1324) returned home with stories of a vast, magnificent empire in eastern Asia.

China is a rich patchwork of landscapes, nationalities, and lifestyles. The life of a peasant at work in a rice field in Fujian province could not be more different from that of the office worker in Beijing, the money trader in Hong Kong, or the Mongol herdsman wandering across the bleak, brown plains of China's north. In China such contrasts can exist side by side. In Hong Kong or Shanghai, old-fashioned markets stand in the shadow of modern high rises. As China rapidly modernizes, many traditional practices continue to flourish alongside the new.

China is a rich mixture of old and new. Here a traditional junk—a sailboat with a virtually flat bottom—sails out of Hong Kong's modern harbor.

FACT FILE

- China shares a land border with 14 neighboring nations: Afghanistan, Bhutan, Burma (Myanmar), India, Kazakhstan, North Korea, Kyrgyzstan, Laos, Mongolia, Nepal, Pakistan, the Russian Federation, Tajikistan, and Vietnam.

- China's name derives from the ancient Qin (pronounced "cheen") dynasty of emperors (221–207 B.C.).

- In Chinese, words are written using symbols called "characters" rather than with letters of an alphabet. In this book Chinese names are shown using letters following a system called Pinyin.

The Chinese flag, modeled on that of the former Soviet Union, is deep red. In the left upper quarter, there is a large, five-point star in gold and four smaller gold stars that curve around it. The large star symbolizes the CCP leadership. The four smaller stars represent the four main groups in society: peasants, workers, bourgeoisie (middle class), and merchants.

China was the first nation in the world to introduce paper money. Today China's paper money is available in 1, 5, 10, 20, 50, and 100-yuan bills.

THE PEOPLE'S REPUBLIC

China's official name is the People's Republic of China. It was adopted on October 1, 1949, after the victory of the Chinese Communist Party (CCP) over the nationalists (*see* pp. 70–71).

China is a totalitarian state—that is, a state in which the government is all-powerful and not responsible to the people—ruled by the CCP. Almost every top civilian, police, and military position, at the national or regional level, is held by a CCP member. The highest office in the CCP is the general secretary, a post held in 1999 by Jiang Zemin (born 1929). Jiang is also China's president and commander-in-chief of the armed forces, the People's Liberation Army (PLA). The political administration is based in the capital, Beijing, which used to be known as Peking in the West.

The Chinese people lack many of the political freedoms that are taken for granted in the West. The CCP nominates all the candidates in elections. The Tiananmen Square massacre of 1989 (*see* p. 77) showed how deeply the CCP is resistant to political reform. Nevertheless, China is undergoing rapid economic reform, moving from a centrally planned economy to a Western-style, market-led one.

The national currency is called renminbi ("people's money"). The unit of this currency is called the yuan (¥). This comprises ten jiao, each of which is made up of ten fen. The former colonies of Hong Kong (Britain) and Macau (Portugal) are now part of China, but both have kept the currency they had under colonial rule: the Hong Kong dollar (HK$) and the Macau pataca (M$).

POPULATION DENSITY

China's population lives mainly in the eastern part of the country, where the land is relatively flat and fertile. The most populous areas of all are around the coastal ports and industrialized zones of central China. The least populated areas are in the mountainous tablelands, deserts, and steppes of China's far west and north.

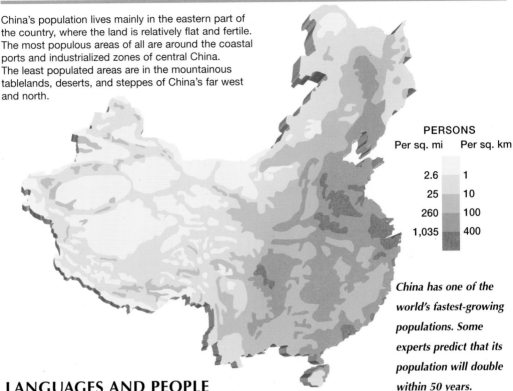

PERSONS

Per sq. mi	Per sq. km
2.6	1
25	10
260	100
1,035	400

China has one of the world's fastest-growing populations. Some experts predict that its population will double within 50 years.

LANGUAGES AND PEOPLE

Some 95 percent of China's inhabitants are Han Chinese. Although the Han Chinese speak different dialects, there is a standard language known as *putonghua* ("common language"), or Modern Standard Language. This is based on the dialect spoken in the capital, Beijing, and is often called Mandarin Chinese in the West.

China is also home to many ethnic groups and nationalities, who number more than 67 million. Most of these live in China's border regions. Among them are Tibetans, Mongols, Uighurs, and Cantonese. These people speak their own language though some also speak a little Mandarin Chinese.

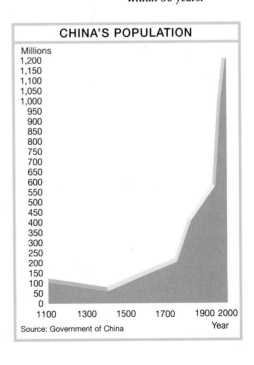

CHINA'S POPULATION

Millions
1,200
1,150
1,100
1,050
1,000
950
900
850
800
750
700
650
600
550
500
450
400
350
300
250
200
150
100
50
0

1100   1300   1500   1700   1900 2000
Year

Source: Government of China

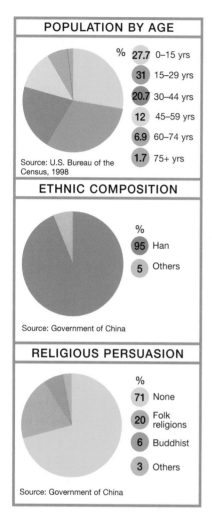

POPULATION BY AGE

%	
27.7	0–15 yrs
31	15–29 yrs
20.7	30–44 yrs
12	45–59 yrs
6.9	60–74 yrs
1.7	75+ yrs

Source: U.S. Bureau of the Census, 1998

ETHNIC COMPOSITION

%	
95	Han
5	Others

Source: Government of China

RELIGIOUS PERSUASION

%	
71	None
20	Folk religions
6	Buddhist
3	Others

Source: Government of China

The charts above show the complex makeup of China's population.

This chart shows where the Chinese people live. Despite the recent industrialization, China remains overwhelmingly agricultural.

China's mostly rugged terrain means that the country's huge population depends upon food grown on just 10 percent of the land. Agriculture is the traditional backbone of China's economy, but in the last ten years, there has been rapid industrialization. In the coastal cities especially, thousands of factories have been built to produce consumer goods for export.

The rapid growth in these cities has attracted great waves of migrants away from rural areas to look for work in the city. However, only about 30 percent of China's population is classified as urban.

China's population is increasing rapidly, and threatens the country's ability to feed itself. In recent years the Chinese have attempted to limit the increase by imposing birth-control measures. Nevertheless, experts predict that China's population will reach 1.4 billion in 2020.

Atheism and Religion

As a communist state, China has no official religion and there is no religious instruction in schools. Nevertheless, religion is not banned; it is only preaching that is forbidden, and religious groups can operate but only within strict limits. Even today, the ancient Chinese philosophies of Confucianism (*see* pp. 50 and 51) and Taoism (*see* p. 50) have many followers.

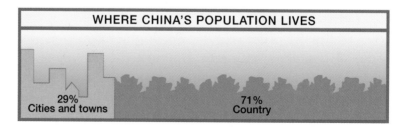

WHERE CHINA'S POPULATION LIVES

29% Cities and towns

71% Country

There are also religions that came from other countries. Islam spread to China soon after it was founded in the early seventh century, and China now has a Muslim population of about 12 million. Buddhism, which originally came from India, appeared in China during the first century A.D. and became an important religion. Christianity arrived in China in the seventh century, but today there are few Christians in China. There is a small Jewish community in Kaifeng. These people may be the descendants of merchants who came to China when Kaifeng was its capital. They no longer practice Jewish rites, but consider themselves to be ethnically Jewish.

The National Anthem

China's national anthem was composed in 1932 and was adopted by the People's Republic in 1949. Its words are full of revolutionary fervor. Tibet has its own national anthem, based on ancient Tibetan sacred music. China does not allow the Tibetan anthem to be sung or played within Tibet.

Arise, you who refuse to be slaves!
With our flesh and blood, let us build our new Great Wall!
The peoples of China live in a time of crisis.
Everybody must roar their defiance.
Arise! Arise! Arise!
Millions of hearts with one mind,
Brave the enemy's gunfire
March on! Brave the enemy's gunfire!
March on! March on!

Pronouncing Chinese

Modern Standard Chinese is often represented in English using the Pinyin system of transliteration. This means that English letters are used to show Chinese sounds. Most of the letters used in the Pinyin system are pronounced much as they are in English. There are some exceptions to this, however:

c	pronounced like *ts*
zh	pronounced like *dj*
q	pronounced like *ch*
x	pronounced like *sh*

Some vowel sounds are also pronounced a little differently:

e	usually like *a* in *ago*
i	usually like *ee* in *bee*
ai	like *eye*
ei	like *ay* in *day*
ao	like *ow* in *how*
ou	like *ow* in *low*

Try pronouncing some of the words that you will find in this book: Mao Zedong (*mow zay-dong*), Qin (*cheen*), Zhengzhou (*djeng-djo*), Xi River (*shee*).

Land and Cities

"So great a number of houses and of people, no one could tell the number...I believe that there is no place in the world to which so many merchants come, or dearer things..."

Venetian traveler Marco Polo (1254–1324), writing about Beijing

It is impossible to understand either China's long history or its rich culture without a knowledge of its geography. From early days, when the first civilizations developed along the country's great river valleys, the history of the Chinese people has been shaped by their country's beautiful and sometimes awesome landscapes.

China is vast. In total China covers an area of 3,691,500 square miles (9,561,000 sq. km), extending 3,100 miles (5,000 km) from north to south and 3,400 miles (5,500 km) from east to west, making it even bigger than the United States. China extends across more than 60 degrees of longitude. This means that the sun rises over the mountainous pasturelands of Xinjiang in China's far west two hours later than it does over subarctic Heilongjiang, China's most northeasterly province.

Within this huge area, there is an astonishing variety of landscapes and climates. In the far north are frozen tundra and steppe, and in the far south, lush, tropical forests. In the far west are towering mountains and vast deserts dotted with fertile oases, and to the east, a patchwork of croplands and rice fields.

Mighty rivers flow eastward from the mountainous west down to China's huge arc of coastline bordering the Pacific Ocean. The coast is indented by about 100 bays with 20 deepwater harbors, most of which remain ice-free all year round.

The craggy peaks and tall rock columns of the Wuling Mountains, Hunan province, tower over the surrounding luxuriant subtropical forest.

FACT FILE

● China covers more than 30 degrees of latitude from north to south.

● The land boundary of China is about 12,400 miles (19,960 km) long, while the coastline extends in a huge arc, 8,700 miles (14,000 km) long.

● China is home to 13 percent of the global total of mammal and bird species. Many species are found only in China, including 72 kinds of mammal and 99 varieties of bird.

● China's most endangered animals include the giant panda (*see* p. 35), the South China tiger, and the Chang river dolphin.

The two highest mountains in China are:

• Everest (on the border with Nepal)—29,028 feet (8,848 m)

• Xixabangma Feng—26,286 feet (8,012 m)

An old fort guards a mountain pass near the Tibetan capital, Lhasa.

THE TERRAIN

About one-third of China's total area comprises mountains or highland areas, while the country's rivers are some of the mightiest in the world. On maps the Chinese words *shan* and *jiang* or *he* are often used to designate the mountain ranges and rivers of the country.

The World's Highest Mountains

People sometimes compare China's terrain to a staircase descending from west to east. The most westerly "step" is dominated by the lofty Tibetan and Qinghai plateaus, The Tibetan Plateau is the highest area on Earth and is sometimes called the "Roof of the World." At the plateau's center, the average elevation is more than 13,120 feet (4,000 m). Some of China's greatest rivers flow from the Tibet and Qinghai plateaus.

At the southern rim of the Tibetan Plateau, on the Nepalese–Tibetan border, are the soaring Himalayan mountains. Here stands the world's tallest peak, Mount Everest, which is 29,028 feet (8,848 m) high. The Chinese call Everest Zmulangmafeng.

China's west is not all lofty mountains, however. In the north is the Tarim Basin, the largest inland basin in the world. Here is the inhospitable Taklimakan Desert and the vast, shifting salt lake, Lop Nur. Farther east, too, is the Turpan Depression. At about 500 feet (150 m) below sea level, this is the second-lowest area on Earth after the Dead Sea. It is the hottest area of China, and the Chinese call it the "Oasis of Fire."

The next step is also a collection of mountains and plateaus but is much lower. This area comprises the

Guizhou–Yunnan Highlands; the mountains of eastern Sichuan and Hubei provinces; the Qinling mountain range; the plateau of Gansu, Shaanxi, and Shanxi; and the plateau of Mongolia. The elevation here is between 3,300 and 6,600 feet (1,000–2,000 m). The fertile Sichuan Basin forms the only important depression. Most of the land in the basin lies below 1,650 feet (500 m).

The lowest step stretches down to the Pacific Ocean and is the most fertile and populous area of China. In the far north, the terrain is low and flat, broken only occasionally by mountains. Farther south are the vast flood plains of China's great rivers. In the far south, there are low mountains crossed by river valleys.

The broad, silt-laden Huang River twists through China's northern lowlands.

China's Great Rivers

China has more than 50,000 rivers, of which the most important are the Huang, Chang, and the Xi. All three rivers have their source in the mountains in the west.

Northernmost is the Huang, or Yellow River, which gets its name from the millions of tons of yellow loess (loamy soil) that it sweeps downstream. The Chinese call the river "China's Sorrow" because of its record of disastrous floods. The Huang rises in Qinghai province. From there it flows eastward to Gansu province, then turns north to form an upside-down "U" as it passes through Inner Mongolia. Then the river turns south again and travels through five provinces on its way to the Yellow Sea.

Although much smaller in volume than the mighty Chang, the Huang River carries nearly three times as much silt. Many dikes (artificial banks) have been built

China's longest rivers are:
• Chang—3,965 miles (6,380 km)
• Huang—3,395 miles (5,464 km)
• Xi—1,323 miles (2,129 km)

The Chinese name Chang Jiang means "long river." Different stretches of the Chang, however, are given other names. At its upper reaches in Yunnan, for example, it is called the Jin Sha Jiang, the "river of golden sand."

in an attempt to control the river. Because so much sand and silt drops to the river bottom, the level of the dikes has to be raised frequently. Downriver, the silt deposits have raised the riverbed as much as 15 feet (4.6 m) above the surrounding countryside. Consequently boats passing along the river sometimes appear to be floating above the surrounding countryside. In late summer and early fall, heavy rainfall upriver sends enormous amounts of water downstream where it often bursts through dikes and sweeps across the countryside.

In addition to being the longest river in China, the Chang is also the most important. It has been a major transportation and trade route to and from eastern China for thousands of years. Together with its tributaries, it accounts for almost half of China's waterways.

The Chang rises on the Tibetan Plateau and passes through winding canyons, underground caverns, and giant lakes before emptying into the East China Sea just north of Shanghai. In its upper reaches—nearly half of its length—the Chang is a mountain torrent and floods in the summer. In 1998 a disastrous summer flood killed some 3,000 people.

The Chang River passes through some spectacular gorges. One Chinese poet compared the Three Gorges in Sichuan province, to "a 1,000 seas poured into one cup."

The Xi River is the major water-transportation route in southern China. The Xi rises in the Guizhou–Yunnan Highlands and flows eastward until it joins the Dong (East) and Bei (North) rivers south of Guangzhou. Together these rivers form the broad Pearl River, the main channel of which joins the South China Sea at the port of Hong Kong (*see* pp. 44–45). The Xi River is much stronger than the Huang River because of the monsoon rains that fall in the south.

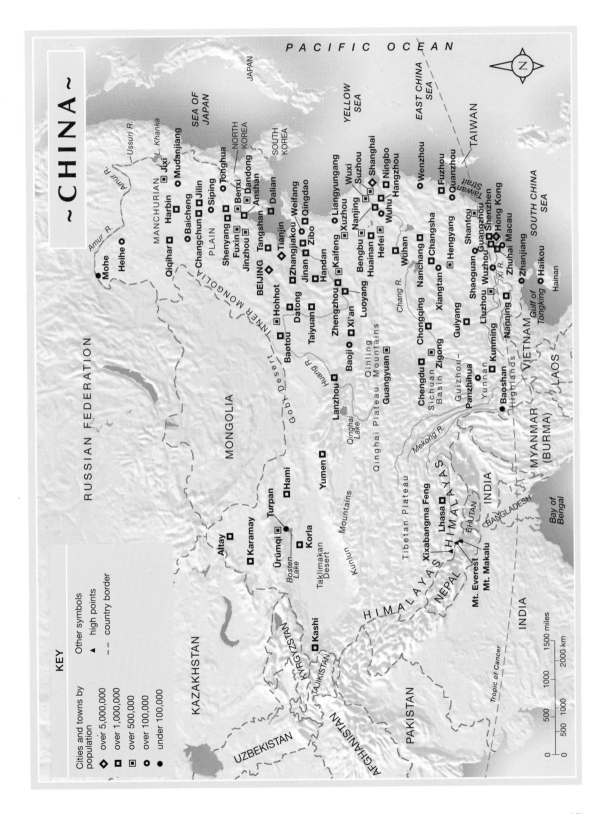

~CHINA~

KEY

Cities and towns by population
- ◇ over 5,000,000
- ■ over 1,000,000
- ▣ over 500,000
- ○ over 100,000
- ● under 100,000

Other symbols
- ▲ high points
- – – country border

PACIFIC OCEAN

RUSSIAN FEDERATION

KAZAKHSTAN

UZBEKISTAN

AFGHANISTAN

TAJIKISTAN

KYRGYZSTAN

PAKISTAN

INDIA

NEPAL

BHUTAN

BANGLADESH

MYANMAR (BURMA)

LAOS

VIETNAM

MONGOLIA

INNER MONGOLIA

MANCHURIAN PLAIN

SEA OF JAPAN

JAPAN

NORTH KOREA

SOUTH KOREA

YELLOW SEA

EAST CHINA SEA

TAIWAN

SOUTH CHINA SEA

Bay of Bengal

Gulf of Tongking

Taiwan Strait

Amur R.
Ussuri R.
L. Khanka

Gobi Desert

Huang R.

Chang R.

Qinling Mountains

Qinghai Plateau

Qinghai Lake

Tibetan Plateau

Sichuan Basin

Guizhou–Yunnan Highlands

Mekong R.

HIMALAYAS

Kunlun Mountains

Taklimakan Desert

Bosten Lake

Xi R.

Tropic of Cancer

Mohe ●
Heihe ●
Qiqihar ■
Harbin ◇
Baicheng ○
Changchun ◇
Jilin ■
Siping ○
Jixi ○
Mudanjiang ○
Tonghua ○
Benxi ■
Fuxin ■
Shenyang ◇
Jinzhou ■
Dandong ○
Anshan ■
Dalian ◇
Hohhot ▣
Baotou ■
Datong ■
Zhangjiakou ■
BEIJING ◇
Tianjin ◇
Tangshan ■
Weifang ■
Zibo ■
Jinan ◇
Qingdao ◇
Handan ■
Taiyuan ◇
Zhengzhou ◇
Kaifeng ■
Xuzhou ×
Liangyungang ○
Nanjing ◇
Suzhou ◇
Shanghai ◇
Wuxi ◇
Ningbo ■
Hangzhou ◇
Wenzhou ○
Fuzhou ■
Quanzhou ■
Bengbu ○
Hefei ■
Huainan ■
Wuhu ■
Wuhan ◇
Luoyang ■
Xi'an ◇
Baoji ■
Guangyuan ○
Lanzhou ◇
Yumen ■
Hami ■
Turpan ●
Ürümqi ●
Korla ■
Karamay ▣
Altay ○
Kashi ■
Chengdu ◇
Chongqing ◇
Nanchang ◇
Changsha ○
Xiangtan ○
Hengyang ○
Shaoguan ○
Guangzhou ◇
Shenzhen ◇
Hong Kong ◇
Macau ◇
Zhuhai ◇
Shantou ○
Liuzhou ■
Wuzhou ■
Nanning ◇
Zhanjiang ○
Haikou ○
Hainan
Guiyang ■
Zigong ◇
Panzhihua ●
Baoshan ●
Kunming ◇
Xishuangbanna
Lhasa ■
Xixabangma Feng ▲
Mt. Everest ▲
Mt. Makalu ▲

N

0   500   1000   1500 miles
0   500 1000 2000 km

PROVINCES AND REGIONS OF CHINA

China is divided into provinces, autonomous (independent) regions, and municipalities. In the late 1990s, Macau and Hong Kong joined China as special administrative regions. The map below shows all China's administrative areas and capitals (marked ●), together with a list of their names.

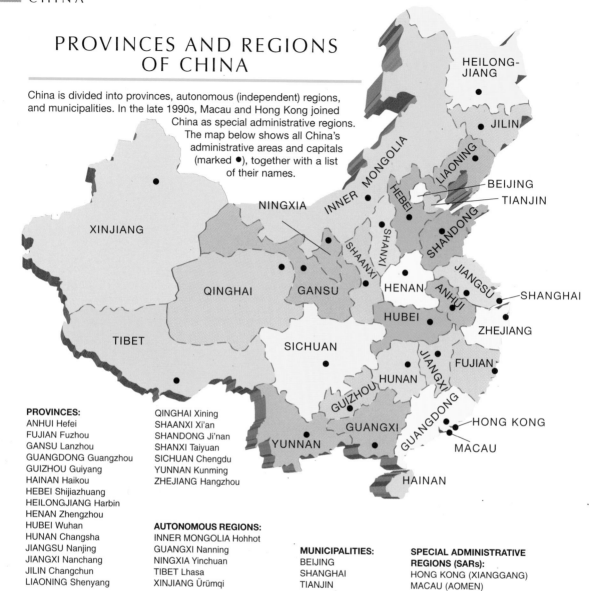

PROVINCES:
ANHUI Hefei
FUJIAN Fuzhou
GANSU Lanzhou
GUANGDONG Guangzhou
GUIZHOU Guiyang
HAINAN Haikou
HEBEI Shijiazhuang
HEILONGJIANG Harbin
HENAN Zhengzhou
HUBEI Wuhan
HUNAN Changsha
JIANGSU Nanjing
JIANGXI Nanchang
JILIN Changchun
LIAONING Shenyang

QINGHAI Xining
SHAANXI Xi'an
SHANDONG Ji'nan
SHANXI Taiyuan
SICHUAN Chengdu
YUNNAN Kunming
ZHEJIANG Hangzhou

AUTONOMOUS REGIONS:
INNER MONGOLIA Hohhot
GUANGXI Nanning
NINGXIA Yinchuan
TIBET Lhasa
XINJIANG Ürümqi

MUNICIPALITIES:
BEIJING
SHANGHAI
TIANJIN

SPECIAL ADMINISTRATIVE REGIONS (SARs):
HONG KONG (XIANGGANG)
MACAU (AOMEN)

PROVINCES AND REGIONS

One of the most difficult challenges facing China's emperors was how to administer their vast, unwieldy empire. The emperors solved the problem by setting up a national civil service that made sure that imperial orders were carried out. If need be, an emperor could also rely on his armies to enforce his rule. When the communists came to power in 1949, they, too, needed a way to make sure that their policies were carried out everywhere, even thousands of miles away from the capital in Beijing. The system that the communists introduced in the early 1950s essentially is in place today.

The People's Republic of China is divided into 22 provinces, five autonomous regions (Tibet, Xinjiang, Inner Mongolia, Guangxi, and Ningxia), three municipalities (Beijing, Shanghai, and Tianjin), and two special administrative regions, or SARs (Hong Kong and Macau). The municipalities and SARs are self-governing. China also claims the island of Taiwan (*see* p. 23), though Taiwan disputes the claim.

The Southwest

China's south and southwest is dominated by the vast, landlocked province of Sichuan, which is roughly the size of Texas. With more than 110 million people, it is China's most populous province. Sichuan's name means "four rivers," after the four great rivers that flow through it, including the mighty Chang. The plentiful rainfall and very fertile soil in Sichuan also make it China's richest agricultural region.

In the east of the province is the Sichuan Basin, also known as the Red Basin. This land depression, covering 75,000 square miles (194,250 sq. km), is sheltered from cold winds by the surrounding mountains. The land is very fertile, and the rice fields can yield two or three harvests each year. In total Sichuan provides 8 percent of China's agricultural output.

To the south of Sichuan, on a spur of the Tibetan Plateau, is the province of Yunnan. There is an astonishing range of landscapes in

The Grand Buddha, at Leshan in Sichuan province, is one of the wonders of China. This 233-foot-high (71 m) statue was carved into the sheer rockface during the Tang dynasty of emperors (A.D. 618–907) and took 90 years to complete. The Buddha's ears are 23 feet (7 m) long and his big toe is 28 feet (8.5 m) long—about the length of a bus!

the province—snowbound mountains, lush rain forest and rice fields, and green river valleys. There is a rich variety of flora and fauna, too. Yunnan has more than 2,500 kinds of wild flowers and plants. In the rain forests of Xishuangbanna in the far south are elephants, tigers, golden-haired monkeys, gibbons, and hornbills.

The province is home to 28 different ethnic groups, including the Dai, Wa, and Lahu. In ancient times a people called the Dian set up a powerful kingdom in the east of the province. They had slaves and practiced human sacrifice. In more recent times, the province has been troubled by the war in Vietnam and by the drugs that flood into China across its border from Myanmar (Burma).

Southeast of Sichuan is another mountainous province, Guizhou. It is one of the poorest and most backward areas in China. Eight million of its 36 million people live below China's poverty level, and almost three-quarters are unable to read or write. Transportation, too, is very poor. Despite its poverty, Guizhou can be a colorful and lively place. The 30 or so groups of minority peoples who live there, such as the Bouyei, Dong, and Muslim Hui, celebrate a huge number of festivals.

The South

In the far south is the autonomous region of Guangxi. Almost a third of Guangxi's population is made up of minority groups, the largest being the Zhuang.

The Chinese sometimes describe this area as "paradise on Earth." Its landscape is made up of jagged peaks, peaceful lakes, underground caverns, and lush plains. This kind of landscape is called karst, and is formed when limestone erodes into unusual shapes, either as towering pinnacles and spires or as caves with underground streams. The climate is hot and wet, and the main crops are rice and sugarcane.

East of Guangxi is the province of Guangdong. From its low-lying hills, many rivers flow down to the province's long coastline on the South China Sea.

The province is dominated by its capital, Guangzhou, which is better known in the West as Canton. The local dialect, Guangdonghua—also known as Cantonese—is the standard speech of the province. Cantonese people are fiercely independent and business-oriented. Over the years they have emigrated all over the world, taking with them their distinctive dialect and cooking style.

Guangdong was the first part of China to be exploited by Europeans, who forced the Chinese to let them trade through many of its ports (*see* pp. 66–67). Hong Kong (*see* pp. 44–45) was a British colony from 1842 to 1997, and Macau was a Portuguese territory from 1557 to 1999.

To the north of Guangdong are the provinces of Jiangxi, Hunan, and Fujian. Jiangxi is famous for its manufacture of porcelain. The industry is based in the town of Jingdezhen, where thousands of people work in kilns and workshops. In the north is the township of Lushan. Its beautiful mountain landscapes have long been an inspiration for China's painters, and many important communist meetings have taken place at the resort.

A peasant carries water along a path in Guangxi province. To the left are rice fields, and in the background are the towering rock pinnacles that are characteristic of the province's karst landscape.

Hunan is a prosperous agricultural region of lush rice fields and spectacularly shaped mountains. It is also China's major tea-producing area. The province is chiefly famous, though, as the birthplace of the great 20th-century Chinese leader Mao Zedong. In the 1960s three million people a year flocked to the tiny village of Shaoshan, where he was born, to pay their respects. Even today many people come to take photographs of Mao's childhood home or to explore the Museum of Chairman Mao. In the museum, visitors can have a computer-generated image made that shows them shaking hands with Mao.

A fisherman goes cormorant-fishing on the Grand Canal in Zhejiang. Cormorant-fishing takes place throughout central and southern China. Fishermen rear young birds to dive into the water and fish for their owners. The birds are prevented from swallowing their prey by the rings tied around their necks. Traditionally the fishermen allow the cormorants to eat every seventh fish as a reward for all their hard work.

The provinces of Fujian and Zhejiang are on China's southern coasts. In ancient times Fujian grew rich by trading silks, porcelain, and precious jewels through its busy ports, such as the capital, Fuzhou. Like the people of Guangdong to the south, people from Fujian have emigrated all over the world. Many of the people who live on the island of Taiwan, off the coast of Fujian, think of the area as their homeland.

Zhejiang is one of China's smallest provinces, but it is also one of its richest. Its fertile northern lands lie in the Chang Delta and are crisscrossed by thousands of irrigation canals. At the southern end of the Grand Canal (*see* p. 91) is Zhejiang's capital, the ancient city of Hangzhou, once the capital of the Song dynasty. When Venetian traveler Marco Polo visited China in the 13th century, he was amazed at the city, praising its "superiority to all others in point of beauty and grandeur." Some of the buildings have been carefully reconstructed, and today tourists flock to the city.

Taiwan

The large tropical island of Taiwan lies 100 miles (160 km) off the coast of Fujian province. Until the 17th century, the island was inhabited by a people who were related to the people of the Philippines, a group of islands that lie to the south. Portuguese navigators visited the island in 1590 and were so impressed by the splendor of its evergreen forests and rugged mountains that they called it Formosa, which means "beautiful."

In the 17th century, Chinese people began to settle on the island. They lived by growing sugar and rice on the fertile plains on the island's western coast. Toward the end of the 19th century, Taiwan officially became a province of China, with its capital at T'ai-pei.

In 1895 Taiwan's near neighbor, Japan, seized the island, but after Japan's defeat at the end of World War II in 1945, Taiwan became part of China again. After the communists came to power on the Chinese mainland in 1949, the nationalists fled to the island and set up a rival government of China in T'ai-pei. For two decades the United States and other noncommunist powers recognized Taiwan as the rightful government of China. Then, in 1971, U.S. President Richard Nixon made a historic visit to Beijing, and most countries of the world followed his lead in recognizing the communist People's Republic as the legitimate (rightful)

government of China. Today Taiwan still lays claim to the Chinese mainland, and China still lays claim to Taiwan and frequently threatens to invade the island. For both Taiwan and China, the island is a province of China.

Supporters of Taiwan's government say that it is the most democratic part of China. In 1996 Taiwan's government held what many called the "first presidential election in Chinese history." Lee Tenghui, already Taiwan's president, was democratically reelected to his position.

Taiwan is prosperous and is one of the world's most densely populated areas. It is a world leader in electronics and has a large fishing fleet.

Zhejiang's coastline is dotted with thousands of islands. There are many busy ports, such as Ningbo and Beicang. The province is famous for its silk and satin textiles and produces one-third of all China's raw silk.

The island of Hainan is an offshore province. Its name means "south sea island," evoking the palm-fringed beaches of this tropical island. The climate is warm, even during the Chinese winter, and yields an abundance of tropical cash crops, including coconuts, pepper, coffee, pineapple, and bananas. On the coast, people also harvest prawns, oysters, and crabs.

The West

On China's northwest border is the Xinjiang Uygur Autonomous Region. It occupies a vast area of 635,000 square miles (1.64 million sq. km) but has a comparatively small population of only 16 million people. The population is very mixed, and includes Han Chinese, Uygur, Kazakhs, and Chinese Muslims (Hui). This desolate area contains the Tarim Basin. Inside this huge area covering 215,000 square miles (556,850 sq. km) lies the Taklimakan Desert, where China tests nuclear weapons.

Xinjiang has abundant mineral resources, with deposits of 122 minerals, including iron, copper, aluminum, and chromium. More than 35 oil and natural-gas fields have been developed in the region. Grasslands in Xinjiang cover 193,050 square miles (500,000 sq. km), which is almost a quarter of China's total grassland area. More than 60 million head of livestock graze on these lands.

The vast, rugged land of Tibet is high up on a plateau that is entirely encircled by mountains. For a long time, Tibet remained a mysterious and hidden

A Kazakh man transports a sheep on horseback through the Tian Shan mountain pastures in Xinjiang province. This remote province is a patchwork of Central Asian peoples, including Muslim Uygurs, Kyrgyz, and Kazakhs.

kingdom because it was so difficult to reach. The present autonomous region of Tibet covers some 471,660 square miles (1,221,600 sq. km)—more than one and a half times the size of Texas. In Chinese the region is known as Xizang.

The small Tibetan population of about 2.3 million people follows a special kind of Buddhism. It was heavily influenced by an old Tibetan religion called Bon, which believed in demons and magic. The traditional spiritual and political leader of the Tibetans is the Dalai Lama. Tibetans believe that each Dalai Lama is the reincarnation of the last. The present Dalai Lama, Tenzin Gyatso, is the 14th and was chosen when he was only two years old.

In its past Tibet has often been under Chinese control but was independent from 1911 until 1950. In 1950 soldiers of the People's Republic of China invaded Tibet. The Chinese government justified this action by saying that the Dalai Lama ruled his people oppressively. Nine years later the Tibetans rebelled, but the Chinese put down the uprising, and the Dalai Lama escaped across the southern border into Nepal. Tibet became an "autonomous" region of China, but Tibetans continue to struggle for their independence. The capital of Tibet is the holy city of Lhasa (*see* pp. 42–43).

Bordering Xinjiang and Tibet is the province of Qinghai, which once was part of Tibet. Qinghai is a vast territory of grassland, tundra, and snowy mountains. The Huang and Chang rivers both have their sources in this province. The local nomadic people keep animals such as cattle, yaks, goats, and sheep on the grasslands.

The snow-capped Mount Kailash is one of the holiest sites in Tibet. Tibetan pilgrims make a complete circuit of the mountain as an act of veneration. This kind of holy journey is called a kora. Here the sacred mountain is seen from Chuku Monastery.

The province is rich in mineral resources. Eighty-three kinds of minerals—including salt, potassium chloride, and magnesium chloride—are found in the province's Qaidam Basin, dubbed the "Treasure Bowl of China."

The Northwest

The Inner Mongolia Autonomous Region (Nei Menggu for Chinese people) forms a great arc of land between China's ancient provinces and the independent country called Mongolia (formerly called Outer Mongolia). The province is mostly grassland. In winter these grasslands are swept by freezing winds and blizzards; summer, though, can be baking hot. The capital of Inner Mongolia is Hohhot, which is known to its Mongolian inhabitants as Kukukhoto.

Together with Mongolia and parts of Siberia, the province is the traditional homeland of the nomadic people called the Mongols. The Mongols were famous horse breeders and traditionally lived in a circular tent made from animal hide called a *ger* (or, in Russian, *yurt*).

The Ming emperors rebuilt the Great Wall (*see* p. 29) across the south of Mongolia in an unsuccessful attempt to keep the Mongols from invading their country. In the

The capital of Mongolia is Hohhot, which means "blue city" in the Mongolian language.

The Mongolian grasslands are dotted with gers—circular tents of animal skin or felt. The gers are home to the nomadic (wandering) Mongols.

13th and 14th centuries, under the leadership of Genghis Khan (*see* p. 61) and his successors, the Mongols built up a mighty empire that stretched west from China to present-day Hungary and south to Vietnam. Since the collapse of the Mongol empire, Russia and China have fought for control of the Mongol homelands. It was only in 1962 that the border between Inner and Outer Mongolia was settled. Today Mongols make up only 15 percent of the total population of Inner Mongolia—the rest are mostly Han Chinese.

Today the Mongol herdsman is more likely to tend his cattle on motorcycle than on horseback.

Southwest of Inner Mongolia, on the "Chinese" side of the Great Wall, are Shaanxi and Ningxia Hui Autonomous Region. Like Mongolia, Ningxia is an independent region and is the homeland of the Hui (Chinese Muslims). Much of the province is desert, except in the northern part, where the Huang River heads south again. Here there is a pleasant landscape of willow-lined canals and green rice fields.

Shaanxi is a mountainous province, split by the Wei and Han rivers. The valley of the Wei River forms a major communication route to Sichuan and the southwest of China. There are huge coal reserves in the north of Shaanxi province, second only to those of the neighboring province of Shanxi. Cotton, wheat, and millet are grown in the valleys of the Wei and Han rivers. The soil is so fertile that it can produce three crops in two years.

The Chinese traditionally regarded the wild and remote province of Gansu as the northern geographic limit of China. The southern part of the province has high mountains, and to the east is the Huang River, on its northward turn toward Mongolia. There are often severe earthquakes in Gansu. In 1920 some 246,000 people died in landslides caused by an earthquake. Whole cities and towns were lost in the disaster.

The capital of Shaanxi is Xi'an on the Wei River. Under different names—Xianyang, Chang'an, and Xi'an—the city was capital to 11 imperial dynasties.

27

The Northeast

China's northernmost province, Heilongjiang, occupies some three-fifths of the vast Manchurian Plain. To the north, east, and west, Heilongjiang is surrounded by mountains. To the north, across the Amur and Ussuri rivers, is Russia. Heilongjiang winters are very cold and long and the Amur, or Heilong, River is frozen for half the year. Together with the neighboring provinces of Jilin and Liaoning, Heilongjiang is one of three provinces that formed the historic land of Dongbei, or Manchuria.

The Manchurian Plain is famous for its rich, black soil, and huge acreages are planted with wheat, corn, sugar beets, and sunflowers. Heilongjiang also has some of the largest gold reserves in the country. Northwest of Heilongjiang's capital, Harbin, is the Daqing Oilfield—one of China's major crude-oil production facilities.

Jilin is south of Heilongjiang. It borders on North Korea to the east and has its capital at Changchun. The province is the historical homeland of the Manchus (*see* p. 64), although many ethnic Koreans also live there. The people live mostly by farming and forestry, although there is a lot of industry, too.

The province's most famous sight is a huge, volcanic lake called Tianchi, meaning "heavenly lake." Lake Tianchi is very deep—ranging from 656 to 1,148 feet (200 to 350 m)—and very cold. The lake lies at the edge of the forested Changbaishan ("everwhite mountain") Reserve, China's largest nature reserve.

The southernmost and most highly developed province of the Manchurian Plain is Liaoning. The provincial capital, Shenyang, was the capital of the Manchus until 1625. Visitors can still see the Manchu Imperial Palace, a complex of 70 buildings with lacquered tiled roofs.

*The often frozen
Amur River divides
Heilongjiang from
Siberian Russia.*

The Great Wall of China

At 3,750 miles (6,035 km) long, the Great Wall of China is the world's longest fortification. Originally the wall was in fact several walls, built to protect the country's most vulnerable borders from invading tribes from the north.

In the third century B.C., China's first emperor, Qin Shihuangdi (259–210 B.C.), had the existing sections of wall joined together. He forced 30,000 peasants and prisoners-of-war to work on the project. So many died during its construction that the wall became known as the "longest cemetery in the world."

Later the wall fell into disrepair, but was rebuilt during the Ming dynasty as a protection against Mongol invasion. Since the end of the Ming dynasty, parts of the wall have crumbled, but large stretches of it near Beijing have been maintained and can be visited by tourists. The mighty edifice is one of 19 UN World Heritage Sites in China.

Today the average height of the remaining segments of wall is 25 feet (7.6 m). The wall is wide enough— 12 feet (3.6 m)—for horsemen to ride along it. There are watchtowers every 300–600 feet (90–180 m).

BEIJING

CHINA

Today Shenyang is the northeast's largest industrial center and China's fourth-largest city. On the tip of the rugged Liandong Peninsula, in the south of Liaoning, is the busy, modern port of Dalian, which the Chinese promote as the Hong Kong of northern China.

——— Qin dynasty
——— Han dynasty
——— Ming dynasty

The map above shows those sections of the Great Wall of China that still stand today. The different colored lines indicate how much of the wall was built during the Qin, Han, and Ming dynasties.

The North Central

The prosperous province of Hebei surrounds Beijing, the capital of China (*see* p. 36), and another major city, Tianjin. In the north is a mountainous tableland. The Great Wall (*see* box) skirts Hebei's northern border, meeting the sea at Shanhaiguan. To the south are flat plains, where wheat and cotton are the principal crops.

Tianjin, China's third-largest city, is set on China's largest artificial harbor and is a key transportation hub for the region. Colorful, hand-woven carpets are one of Tianjin's most famous exports.

To the southeast of Hebei, bordering the Yellow Sea, is the province of Shandong. Throughout its history, Shandong has been vulnerable to floods, which devastated its towns and villages. Ji'nan, the capital, is called the "city of springs" because it has more than a hundred natural springs. More recently another kind of liquid has made Shangdong rich. Shengli Oilfield in Shandong province is the second-largest producer of oil in China.

Thousands of Chinese visit Shandong to climb Taishan Mountain, the most revered of China's five sacred Taoist mountains. To reach the summit and the temples clustered there, visitors must climb up 6,666 steps.

Across the Taihang Mountains from Hebei is the mountainous province of Shanxi, one of the oldest centers of Chinese civilization. Cereal crops were grown here as long ago as 3000 to 5000 B.C. Later the province played a vital role in defending China against Mongol invaders. Today governments are exploiting Shanxi's mineral wealth, and the province supplies one-third of China's iron and coal deposits. Taiyuan, the capital, is an industrial center producing steel, chemicals, and textiles.

Scholars often call the small province of Henan the cradle of Chinese civilization. Some of China's oldest cities grew up around the Huang River, which crosses the province's northern tip. Today Henan is one of China's most densely populated provinces. Most of its population are farmers, who produce mostly cotton, tobacco, and silk.

Shandong province is famous as the birthplace of both Confucius and his follower Mencius, the thinkers who developed China's great philosophy-religion, Confucianism.

Henan's capital, Zhengzhou, is one of the oldest cities in the world. It was founded 3,500 years ago as the capital of the mighty Shang dynasty of emperors.

The Middle and Lower Chang Valley

Most of the province of Hubei lies north of the great Chang River and forms the heartland of China. Highlands in the west rapidly give way to a vast, lowland plain dotted with lakes, where most of the province's population lives. The plain is given over almost entirely to rice-growing. The lively industrial city of Wuhan is Hubei's capital and is the most important inland port of China.

East of Hubei is the province of Anhui, meaning "beautiful peace." A journey across the northern half of the province would be something like crossing the American Midwest, but the southern part of the province is mountainous and divided by the Chang River. The beautiful Huang ("yellow") Mountains, famous for their craggy peaks, wind-gnarled pines, and cloud-strewn skies, are in southern Anhui.

For a long time, Anhui had little industry, but today its people are beginning to exploit its rich resources of copper, iron, and coal. Hefei, the provincial capital, has become an industrial city and mining center.

On the coast, northeast of Anhui, is Jiangsu, China's most fertile province. On the banks of the Chang River is one of China's most ancient cities, Nanjing. Several times in China's history Nanjing was the country's capital, but now it is the capital of Jiangsu province.

This region has a lot of industry, ranging from steelworks to textile production. Freshwater Lake Taihu in the far south of the province is a popular tourist attraction and is also home to a prosperous fishing industry. In the southeastern corner of Jiangsu is the port city of Shanghai.

This village in Anhui province clings to the mountainside as it sweeps down to the Chang River. The stretch of the Chang River in Anhui is famous for its natural beauty and as the home of the rare Chang river dolphin, or baiji.

CHINA'S CLIMATE

China extends through an astonishing range of climatic zones, from the subarctic Heilongjiang in the north to the tropical island of Hainan in the south, from Siberian frosts in the center to steamy heat in the southeast.

The charts below show the seasonal weather patterns of two of China's most important cities. Beijing, in the north, has warm, wet summers and cold winters. Guangzhou, in the south, has a humid, subtropical climate.

China is divided broadly into northern and southern temperature zones along the Chang River. In the south, temperatures seldom fall below freezing, so people can grow crops all year round, including staples such as rice, tea, and sugar. In northern provinces the weather can be bitterly cold and dry. Cereals, peas, and beans are the main crops in the north, although hand-irrigation and plowing are necessary for growing winter wheat.

Summer and Winter

In winter, the temperature difference between the extreme north and far south of China can be as much as 90°F (50°C). In January temperatures in China's northernmost provinces of Heilongjiang and Mongolia can drop as low as -40°F (-40°C). By contrast, on the island of Hainan, in the South China Sea, temperatures fall to just 72°F (22°C).

The prevailing (dominant) winds from the north are very dry and cold and bring little rain, which means that during Heilongjiang's long, hard winters, there are clear days with low temperatures and little rain. In the south, winters are shorter but have regular drizzle and overcast skies.

In summer the range of temperatures between north and south is quite small. Between Beijing and Hong Kong in July,

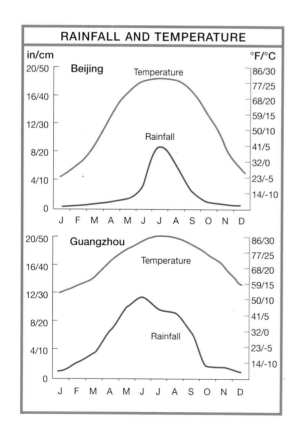

RAINFALL AND TEMPERATURE

the temperature difference is only about 5°F (3°C). In the central region around the Chang River, the summers are long, hot, and humid. Because the weather can be so unbearable in the central region, the Chinese call the three major cities of the area, Wuhan, Chongqing, and Nanjing, "the three furnaces." The hottest place in China is Turpan, in Xinjiang, where temperatures can rise to a blistering 117°F (47°C).

Changing Seasons

One of the few areas to enjoy a seasonal rhythm, with the seasons evenly spaced, is in the lower reaches of the Huang River, where agriculture in China first developed thousands of years ago. In other areas the difference between seasons is often less obvious. In Heilongjiang there is hardly any summer, while in southern Guangdong, there is no winter.

Spring is one of the best times to visit China. Not only is the weather more likely to be mild, but there are magnificent displays of blossom, such as these cherry trees.

Rainfall decreases from southeast to northwest. In the southeast, along the southern and eastern coasts, the summer brings frequent typhoons, or tropical cyclones. These usually strike between May and November but are most frequent in July, August, and September. Although Tibet is called the "Land of Snows," this region is surprisingly arid and can sometimes suffer from intense sandstorms.

Another seasonal feature is the melting of the snows in the Tibetan Plateau. This huge rush of water can cause severe floods in the lower reaches of the Chang, Huang, and Xi rivers, wiping out crops and even destroying whole villages. In many areas of China, successful harvests may depend on the amount of rain in spring. Too much rainfall during this crucial season can destroy crops; too little means drought.

ANIMALS AND PLANTS

Given China's size, it is hardly surprising that the country has a great diversity of natural vegetation, ranging from cacti in the northern deserts to mangrove swamps in the south and alpine flowers in the Himalayan mountains. All in all China has some 30,000 seed-plant species. In a single nature reserve in Sichuan province, there are some 4,000 native plants. More than 200 of these are found only in China.

Many of China's 2,500 species of forest trees are used commercially. Camphor from camphor trees, for instance, is used in the manufacture of celluloid and as an insect repellent. The resin of the lacquer trees provides a varnish for protecting and decorating wooden lacquerwork.

China has 1,174 known species of birds, 420 species of animals, and 500 reptiles and amphibians. There are more than 700 nature reserves, protecting almost 7 percent of China's land. The country's most famous animal, the giant panda bear (*see* box opposite), lives in the bamboo forests of Sichuan and Yunnan. In other mountain areas, the goat antelope, or takin, can be found.

Other species unique to China include the white-lipped deer, the golden-haired monkey, the white-finned porpoise, and the brown-eared pheasant. Many animals, such as tigers and bears, are under threat of extinction because the Chinese use parts of the animals' bodies in some traditional medicines.

The chrysanthemum grows wild in China's subtropical south, particularly in Yunnan, often called the "Kingdom of Flowers."

In the cold far northeast of China, animals such as reindeer, moose, musk deer, bears, and sables can be found. Elsewhere in the country, although not unique to China, are the Manchurian tiger, the red-crowned crane, and the long-armed ape (gibbon).

The Giant Panda

China's most cherished symbol is the giant panda, which the Chinese call a "national treasure." Apart from the occasional fish, the panda eats only the shoots of the fountain bamboo that grows in the forests of Sichuan, Yunnan, and Tibet.

There are now only between 700 and 1,000 pandas left alive in the wild. The giant panda is threatened not only because poachers want its skin but also because its habitat is being gradually destroyed as bamboo forests are cleared to make way for crops or new homes.

Chinese efforts to save this shy animal are focused on the Wolong and Juizhaigou nature reserves in the western part of Sichuan. Security in these reserves is strict. Many poachers have been caught, and even executed, for killing giant pandas.

CHINA'S CITIES

China has some of the oldest cities in the world. The former imperial capital of Chang'an (now Xi'an), for example, once vied with the ancient cities of Rome and Constantinople (modern Istanbul) in its size and splendor.

In the 20th century, many of China's cities have been destroyed by war or torn down during the rule of Mao Zedong. The urban environment has also been badly damaged by pollution, while rapid industrialization over the past half century has caused many cities to sprawl uncontrolled. Today there are more than 40 cities with a population of more than one million. Shanghai is the largest, with more than 14 million residents.

Chinese city streets are sometimes called *dajie* (avenue) and sometimes *lu* (road). A major road or avenue can be split along compass points: *dong* (east), *xi* (west), *bei* (north), and *nan* (south).

One of Beijing's most famous sights is the Tiananmen Gate, or "Gate of Heavenly Peace," which leads into the Forbidden City (see p. 40). In imperial times the emperor came here to address his people. It was here, too, that Mao Zedong proclaimed the People's Republic of China in 1949. Today the gate has a gigantic portrait of China's greatest communist leader.

Beijing: The "Northern Capital"

Under different names Beijing has been China's capital almost continuously since the 13th century, when the Mongol leader Kublai Khan (*see* p. 61) ruled a vast empire from the city. After the collapse of the Mongol empire in the 15th century, the Chinese emperor, Yong Le, moved his government north to Beijing from Nanjing, the "southern capital." The emperor called his new capital Beijing, which means "northern capital."

For a short period between 1928 and 1949, Nanjing was the capital of China again. When the communists took over, Beijing became the capital once more. At that time Beijing was a city famous for its wide-open spaces and wooded hills. Mao Zedong wanted to transform the city from an imperial center into a showcase for communism. On his orders lawns were dug up, the city walls were torn down, and most of the old courtyard homes were demolished. In their place the communists built avenues, high-rise buildings, and factories.

Beijing grew rapidly. Today the city spreads over the northern end of the North China Plain and covers around 16,800 square miles (43,500 sq. km). It is a *sheng* (municipality) and is administered directly by the government. There are 10 *ch'u* (urban districts) and eight *hsien* (rural districts). With more than 12.5 million residents, Beijing has the second-largest population in China. More recently the government has tried to limit the building of new factories in Beijing and to preserve the ancient monuments that survived Mao's policies.

Today the city is still the place where all the decisions affecting the rest of the country are made. In Beijing's busy center, modern and traditional elements combine. There are broad avenues and impressive government buildings, high-rise apartment houses and luxury hotels, as well as the remains of ancient palaces and mansions, and older residential quarters with winding alleyways, or *hutongs*. Away from the downtown area, there are suburbs made up of factories and workers' dormitories. Four huge ring roads carry traffic around the outside of the city.

The people of Beijing are very proud of their city. Beneath the modern surface, the old city is still very much alive. Young people like to stroll in the city's many parks or to visit the outlying historic sites, such as the beautiful Summer Palace. Older people chat in the teahouses or drink the strong liquor known as *mao tai* in taverns. Grandparents, parents, and children all live together, even if housing conditions in the city are cramped.

The best way to get around in Beijing is by subway, which first opened in 1969 and which the Chinese soon called the "Underground Dragon." Subway trains are very crowded but are fast in comparison to buses. The buses are always full and travel very slowly because of the huge volume of traffic on Beijing's roads.

Beijing's Parks

Beijing is famous for its beautiful parks. In imperial times many of these parks were places where the emperor and his court came to walk or to watch fireworks. Now the parks are open to everyone. Jingshan and Beihai parks both lie close to the Forbidden City. From Jingshan Park there is a stunning view southward over the glinting golden palace roofs. Beihai ("north lake") Park is said to have been the site of Kublai Khan's palace, although nothing remains of it. The park is a landscape of artificial hills, with temples, and pavilions.

BEIJING SUBWAY

East–West Line
Circle Line

PINGGUOYUAN

Guchengliu · Bajiaocun · Babaoshan · Yuquanlu · Wukesong · Wanshoulu · Gongzhufen · Junshibowuguan · Muxidi · Nanlishilu · Changchun Jie · Xuanwumen · Hepingmen · Qianmen · Chongwenmen · Beijing Zhan · Unnamed · Unnamed · Unnamed

FUXINGMEN · Xidan · Unnamed · Unnamed · Unnamed · JIANGUOMEN

Chegongzhuang · Xizhimen · Fuchengmen · Jishuitan · Gulou · Andingmen · Yonghegong · Dongzhimen · Dongsishitao · Chaoyangmen

The subway is an easy and safe way to get around Beijing. The subway was opened in 1969, and until 1980 only Chinese people could use it. There are two lines—the Circle and East–West lines. Some stations do not have names.

Many of Beijing's inhabitants prefer to get around their city by bike, weaving in and out of the traffic and around market stalls and street performers. Cyclists cross traffic junctions in groups, hoping for safety in numbers. If they are brave and quick enough, tourists often find that the best way to see the city's sights is on a bicycle.

Despite its haphazard appearance, Beijing is in fact laid out in a very orderly manner. Its traditional gridlike structure, at the center of which stood the Forbidden City, reflected the power of the emperor.

The people of Beijing love food. Restaurants reflect the full range of Chinese cuisine, from the lightly spiced, elegant Cantonese dishes of the south to the rich Mongolian stews of the far north. The most famous dish of the city, though, is succulent Beijing duck. Today there are even fast-food restaurants. The first hamburger restaurant opened in 1992 and was an instant success. It became a fashionable place to go among the most privileged members of Beijing society.

BEIJING CENTER

DI'ANMEN DAJIE

BEIHAI PARK

JINGSHAN PARK

N

WENJIN JIE   JINGSHAN QIAN JIE

FUYOU JIE

BEICHIZHI DAJIE

NANHEYAN DAJIE

The Forbidden City

Zhongnanhai Lake

ZHONGSHAN PARK

Tiananmen Gate

CHANG'AN JIE

TIANAN-MEN SQUARE

CHAN'AN JIE

Great Hall of the People

Museum of Chinese History and Museum of the Revolution

Chairman Mao Mausoleum

QIANMEN DAJIE

A Walk Through Beijing

The Chinese emperors laid out their capital city very carefully. All the buildings, parks, and streets were arranged on a north–south axis. At the central point of this axis was the moated and walled Forbidden City, where the powerful emperor and his court lived.

The Forbidden City got its name because, for 500 years, ordinary Chinese people were forbidden to enter the palace on pain of death. The emperors lived almost exclusively within the city. They were hidden away and separate from the outside world and ruled their country through powerful court officials. Today, though, thousands of tourists stroll through the Forbidden City every year.

The original palace was built in just 15 years at the beginning of the 15th century. Over the years, though, the palace caught fire several times. Fires were usually caused by stray sparks from a firework display or a lantern. Once, in 1664, Manchu warlords stormed the palace and deliberately burned it to the ground, together with its priceless treasures. Finally, in 1949, nationalist troops fighting the communists looted the palace and shipped many of its remaining treasures to the island of Taiwan, where today they are displayed in the National Palace Museum in the capital, T'ai-pei.

The Forbidden City remains one of the most impressive monuments to traditional Chinese architecture. There are six palaces, each with an elegant, polished roof supported by red pillars. The palaces are filled with

Perhaps a million laborers and 100 skilled craftsmen worked to build the original Forbidden City.

Altogether the Imperial City has more than 800 buildings and 9,000 rooms.

THE FORBIDDEN CITY

1 Today a visitor to the Forbidden City enters through the massive Wumen Gate, but in imperial times, only the emperor could use the gate. On ceremonial occasions he would appear flanked by a guard of elephants.

2 Having entered the Wumen Gate, the visitor enters a vast paved courtyard through which a narrow stream flows—the Golden Water Stream. Five marble bridges cross the stream.

3 Straight ahead is the Taihemen, the Gate of Supreme Harmony, guarded by a row of fierce-looking lions. The gate leads into an even bigger courtyard, where the emperor held court. Soldiers entered the courtyard from side gates on the west and civilians from gates on the east. At times as many as 100,000 people gathered here and had to keep absolute silence while the emperor sat on his throne.

4 Directly ahead, and reached by a white marble ramp decorated with dragons, is the spectacular Taihedian, the Hall of Supreme Harmony. This was the emperor's throne room during important state occasions, such as the coronation.

Gardens

Golden Water Stream

Palace of Peace and Longevity

Gardens

Kitchens

Library

Moat

N

5 The smaller Zhonghedian, or Hall of Middle Harmony, was where the emperor received his children and foreign visitors.

6 Next is the Baohedian, the Hall of the Preservation of Harmony, where banquets and civil-service examinations used to be held.

7 Next are the three palaces that made up the imperial living quarters. The most spectacular is the Qianquinggong, or the Palace of Heavenly Purity. In front of the palace are incense burners.

treasures from China's past, including paintings, bronzes, and ceramics. There is even a museum of clocks, which were collected by an emperor.

Surrounding the Forbidden City is the old Imperial, or Inner, City. The court officials lived here, in rectangular, one-story dwellings surrounding a central courtyard. Many of these houses still survive, although several families now share each house.

The focus of the former Imperial City, and the heart of modern Beijing, is the vast Tiananmen Square. It takes its name from the Gate of Heavenly Peace. When the communists redeveloped Beijing in 1958, the square was rebuilt four times bigger. Usually the square is a place where people come to stroll on summer evenings, to fly kites, to exchange gossip, or to cool off after a hard day's work. In 1989, however, tanks brutally broke up pro-democracy demonstrations here (see p. 77).

Many of Beijing's most famous monuments and buildings are on the square. On the north side, leading toward the Forbidden City, is the Tiananmen Gate. In the southwestern corner is the huge Great Hall of the People, which is the seat of the National People's Congress (*see* p. 79). In front of the Great Hall are the People's Heroes Monument and the Chairman Mao Mausoleum. The Heroes Monument is a granite obelisk (a four-sided pillar topped by a pyramid) that stands 118 feet (36 m) high. It was completed on May 1, 1958, to commemorate the heroes of the Chinese Revolution.

The mausoleum was erected in 1976 shortly after Mao's death. Inside the mausoleum Mao's embalmed (preserved) body is displayed in a glass tomb. Every day hundreds of Chinese people file past the tomb to pay their respects to Mao, who for most Chinese people remains a great hero. Nearby street vendors sell a vast array of Mao memorabilia, including towels, keyrings, and even thermometers.

On the eastern side of the square is a somber building that houses both the Museum of Chinese History and the Museum of the Chinese Revolution. The Museum of Chinese History gives an account of world history up to 1919 from a communist perspective. There are displays of weapons, everyday objects, and musical instruments. The Museum of the Revolution tells the story of China after 1919 and the development of the Chinese Communist Party.

Every day at sunrise, soldiers from the People's Liberation Army (PLA) parade as the Chinese flag is raised. The soldiers march at a very precise rate—108 paces per minute.

The vast Tiananmen Square covers 100 acres (40.5 ha), and up to a million or more people can fit in the square. This photo is taken from the Tiananmen Gate and looks southward to the Heroes Monument and the Mao Zedong Mausoleum.

LHASA

LINGKOR BEI LU

Temple

Temple

Temple

Potala

BEIJING ZHONG LU

BEIJING DONG LU

Temple

DOSENGGE LU

KHARNGA DONG LU

LINGKUO DONG LU

People's Park

YUTHOK LU

Jokhang Temple

BARKHOR SQUARE

Mosque

Nunnery

CHINGDOL ZHONG LU

CHINGDOL DONG LU

N

Kyichu River

Lhasa: Tibet's Ancient Capital

The Tibetan capital, Lhasa, falls into two parts. Around the Jokhang Temple is the old Tibetan city, while at the foot of the Potala is the modern Chinese city, which was developed after the Chinese invasion of 1951.

The ancient capital of Tibet, Lhasa, is one of the world's most astonishing cities. It is the traditional home of Tibetan Buddhism and of the Dalai Lamas, the priest-kings of Tibet who once ruled the country from the spectacular Potala Fortress.

Lhasa lies on the Kyichu River, high up on the Tibetan Plateau. In the city's old town, lofty fortresses and golden-roofed temples rise over narrow streets, and whitewashed houses are bright with their painted woodwork. Day and night the streets are crowded with pilgrims—maroon-robed monks, fur-clad Tibetan nomads, called Goloks, and women spinning prayer-wheels.

Lhasa's recorded history goes back to the seventh century A.D., when a young warrior king named Songtsen Gampo united Tibet for the first time and made the city his capital. Songtsen Gampo was so powerful that he was able to marry a Chinese princess. The princess converted her husband to Buddhism, and the king built the Jokhang Temple to house the princess's statue of Buddha. The king also built the princess a mighty fortress, the Potala.

Lhasa's name means "ground of the gods" and was given to the capital by Songsten Gampo.

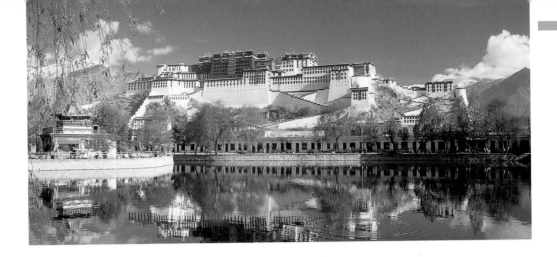

Today the 13-story Potala dominates Lhasa, but it is not the original fortress of Tibet's first king. The present Potala was built mainly by the fifth Dalai Lama in the 17th century. The fortress has more than 1,000 rooms, including hundreds of lamp-lit shrines. The building was built to withstand earthquakes: Its builders poured molten copper into its foundations to strengthen its walls.

At the heart of the Old City is Jokhang Temple, the most holy place for Tibetan Buddhists. According to legend, King Songtsen Gampo threw a ring into the air and promised to build a temple wherever it landed. The ring fell into a lake, and accordingly the king's laborers filled in the lake and built the first Jokhang Temple. The present temple has a beautiful painted cloister and numerous half-lit shrines. Everywhere there is the murmur of monks reciting their mantras (prayers). In the shrines, monks leave gifts of yak butter to burn in the flickering lamps, or white scarves.

Encircling the Jokhang is the Barkhor, a kind of holy square. A stream of pilgrims makes its way around the temple, repeatedly lying face down in the dust. According to Buddhist custom, all the pilgrims move in a clockwise direction. The Barkhor also serves as Lhasa's main marketplace. People gather here to shop, gossip, and watch the street performers.

The Potala Fortress, long the home of the Dalai Lamas, stands on a craggy hill overlooking Lhasa.

Tibetan Buddhist monks can be seen in Barkhor Square. They wear maroon-colored robes and wear orange hats like snail shells.

Hong Kong Island became a British colony in 1842. In 1898 China gave Britain a 99-year lease on the mainland territory to the north of the island.

The Special Administrative Region (SAR) of Hong Kong consists of the Kowloon Peninsula and its offshore islands. Altogether Hong Kong covers 422 square miles (1,092 sq. km), and has a population of some six million.

Hong Kong: China's New City

The city of Hong Kong is unlike any other in China. For more than 100 years, the city and the surrounding territory were a colony of Britain. During that time the city prospered and became a major international port and East Asia's most important financial center. On the surface at least, the city came to look like many other major cities in the West. The city skyline sprouted hundreds of skyscrapers and the city's streets became jammed with shops selling every kind of consumer goods.

On July 1, 1997, however, Britain handed Hong Kong back to China. By agreement between the two nations, Hong Kong became a Special Administrative Region of China. For 50 years, the agreement said, Hong Kong would be allowed to keep its capitalist system and its currency, the Hong Kong dollar. The agreement's slogan was "One country, two systems."

Many people in Hong Kong are nervous about their new rulers. They worry that the Chinese government will restrict their freedom and that the city will lose its prosperity. At first, though, there were few visible changes. Notably a new flag—a white flower with five red stars on a red field—has replaced Britain's Union Jack, and a new train service connects the city with Beijing.

The territory of Hong Kong is divided into four parts: Hong Kong Island itself, the very densely populated mainland area of Kowloon, the largely rural New Territories that lie to the north, and the outlying islands.

HONG KONG SAR

GUANGDONG
--- Provincial border
— Main roads
Built-up areas
NEW TERRITORIES
Kowloon Peninsula
Tao Po
10,000 Buddha Monastery
Tai Mo Peak
Tuen Mun
Shatin
Sai Kung Peninsula
Pearl River Estuary
Trappist Monastery
Peng Chau Island
KOWLOON
HONG KONG
Kai Tak
South China Sea
Lantau Island
Victoria Peak
HONG KONG ISLAND
Po Lin Monastery
Aberdeen
Cheung Chau Island (CT)
Repulse Bay
Lamma Island
N

The bustling city proper clings to the steep northern coast of the mountainous Hong Kong Island. The inhabitants call this area simply "Central." Beneath the soaring skyscrapers are narrow streets and alleys, some of which are closed to automobiles and are crammed with shops and stalls. Ancient-looking double-decker trams carry tourists and inhabitants around the city. The famous Peak Tram climbs to the top of Victoria Peak, from which there is a stunning view over the city and across the harbor.

The southern coast of Hong Kong Island has beach resorts such as the beautiful Repulse Bay and the old fishing village of Aberdeen, where many of Hong Kong's inhabitants have weekend homes.

The city of Hong Kong spills across the harbor to the Kowloon Peninsula. Here, there are many museums, hotels, bars, and restaurants. The New Territories stretch out to the north and northwest of Kowloon. In their hills and mountains are peaceful monasteries and temples, old walled villages, and modern, lively towns.

All in all, there are some 235 islands dotting the waters around Hong Kong. Most are uninhabited, but four—Cheung Chau, Lamma, Lantau, and Peng Chau—have large communities. The islands are often packed with people on vacation.

Hong Kong's spectacular skyline rivals that of Manhattan Island. Nevertheless, the city is a striking mixture of old and new and of traditional Chinese and Western cultures.

Past and Present

"This is a Great Wall and only a great people with a great past could have a great wall..."

Twentieth-century U.S. president Richard M. Nixon

China is one of the world's most ancient nations, with a recorded history that stretches back more than 4,000 years. For centuries China was ruled as a great empire by dynasties of powerful emperors and remained largely untouched by the Western world.

Over the centuries, China was able to develop an advanced civilization, producing astonishing inventions and remarkable works of art. China's single-minded independence, however, left it unable to deal with the European world. The Chinese emperors refused to allow any political, social, or economic change, and China stagnated. In the 18th century, European technology overtook that of China, and the country was unable to resist the influence of the European traders then landing on its shores.

The pressure from European countries sent China into a rapid decline. The Chinese people grew dissatisfied with the arrogance of their emperors' rule, and in 1911 a revolution overthrew the last emperor and a republic was declared. Later, in 1949, after a devastating civil war, the Chinese communists established a People's Republic.

The communists swept away many of the traditions of the imperial era, and China changed from being an agricultural economy into a country with international influence and huge industrial power. This remarkable transformation was achieved only at the cost of terrible suffering and the death of tens of millions of people.

The Great Wall of China, stretching from the Pacific deep into the Gobi Desert, was built to protect the empire from the "barbarians" to the north.

FACT FILE

- China was first unified in 221 B.C., making it one of the world's oldest surviving nations, alongside Egypt, Greece, and India.

- The names of China's dynasties were not the personal names of the imperial families. Sometimes the name is that of the region from which the family came; sometimes it is the title the family held before reaching the throne. In the case of the last three dynasties, the names had symbolic meanings.

- Ruling emperors were never called by their personal names but by a reign title, which usually had a lucky meaning.

Beijing Man

In 1927 archaeologists discovered fossilized human bones while excavating in a cave at Zhoukoudian, southwest of Beijing. Experts dated the remains to about 600,000 B.C. and named them "Beijing Man," or *Homo erectus pekinensis* in Latin. Further excavations uncovered the remains of another 40 or so people, together with tools and ornaments and the bones of animals now extinct.

Beijing Man belonged to an earlier stage of evolution than modern humans (*Homo sapiens*). He was shorter and had three-quarters the brain capacity. Experts deduced from the finds that he used crude stone tools, including scrapers, choppers, and pointed instruments. He ate nuts and berries and could also make fire and use it to cook food.

The caves at Zhoukoudian are a World Heritage Site. Many of the fossils in the area were destroyed during the Japanese invasion of China, but more recently archaeologists have unearthed further exciting finds.

ANCIENT TIMES

The Chinese say that their civilization stretches back some 5,000 years. They have many colorful legends about their country's first rulers. Their first king, they tell, was the god Fuxi, who had the upper body of a man and the tail of a dragon. His wife, Nügua, shaped the first humans out of clay, and Fuxi taught them to hunt and fish, raise animals, and breed silkworms.

Archaeological researchers tell us that China's earliest known inhabitants lived as long ago as 600,000 B.C. The fossilized remains of the "Beijing Man" (*see* box opposite) are the most famous evidence for these early peoples.

About 9,000 years ago, various Neolithic (New Stone Age) cultures grew up along the Huang River and along the east and southeast coast. Those living in the east and south grew rice, while those on China's central plains cultivated another cereal called millet.

The northern people made pots decorated with pictures of fish and birds or with patterns, such as spirals or whorls, and produced the first silks. This complicated process involved breeding a variety of moth that makes itself a silken cocoon when it is a caterpillar. Silk thread was spun from the cocoons and woven into cloth.

The Xia Dynasty

By 2000 B.C. people living in northern China were living in more complex societies. Some of them lived in walled settlements. They used metal tools and developed a written script that became the basis for Chinese

CHINA'S FIRST CULTURES

Longshan Culture

The people of this culture lived on the east China coast by the Yellow Sea. They were excellent farmers and grew vast quantities of rice. They made blackish pottery that was generally less fine than that made by the Yangshao people. This culture gets its name from the village of Longshan, Shandong province.

Yangshao Culture

This culture developed on the plains of north China around the Huang River valley. The culture is named after the village of Yangshao, Henan province, where China's first Neolithic site was discovered in 1920. These people used polished stone hoes, spades, and knives to grow and harvest millet. They also kept dogs and pigs. They made beautiful red pottery, which they decorated with images of fish, birds, and flowers. They may even have developed an early form of writing.

Southeastern Culture

This culture developed in an area that roughly includes the modern provinces of Fujian, Guangdong, and Guangxi, as well as the island of Taiwan. The people here hunted with spears and fished with harpoons, but also planted crops, possibly including rice. Their culture was influenced by that of the peoples of Southeast Asia.

Map labels: MONGOLIA, Zhoukoudian, Huang R., Yellow Sea, Zhengzhou, Chang R., Taiwan, South China Sea, SOUTHEAST ASIA, N

writing. According to legend China's first imperial dynasty, the Xia, ruled at this time. The first Xia emperor, Yu the Great Engineer, was said to have built the country's first canals. Scholars disagree whether the Xia actually existed, but traditionally this great dynasty was overthrown by the Shang about 1650 B.C.

From about 9000 B.C., three major Neolithic cultures developed in China. This map shows the areas in which each culture flourished.

The Shang Dynasty

The Shang kings form the first Chinese imperial dynasty that left behind historical records. This dynasty ruled an area around the Huang River in western Shandong, Hebei, and Henan from about 1650 to 1050 B.C. The people ruled by the kings thought of them as being like gods. They buried them in elaborate underground tombs, together with sacrificed slaves and warriors.

The first Shang capital was at Zhengzhou, in present-day Henan, where the kings ruled over a population made up largely of farmers. The rulers lived in vast

The Xia, Shang, and Zhou dynasties are together known as the "Three Dynasties."

This Shang-dynasty bronze cauldron was found in Shanxi province. It was used to hold wine on ceremonial occasions.

Believers in Taoism follow the Tao ("the Way"). Taoism was developed by the hermit Lao Zi, who lived at the same time as Confucius. The central principle of Taoism is *wu wei*, which means acting in accordance with nature.

walled settlements that included suburbs and industries. Experts have calculated that it would have taken 10,000 workers 18 years to build Zhengzhou's mighty walls.

During the Shang dynasty, the Chinese began to use bronze for the first time. Rather than working the metal with a hammer on an anvil, they poured molten bronze into molds made from pottery. Using this method they were able to make not just knives and axes but huge ceremonial containers. The largest container found, a rectangular cauldron, measures 52 inches (132 cm) high, 43 inches (109 cm) long, and 30 inches (76 cm) wide. The king and the nobles used horse-drawn chariots with bronze fittings when they went to hunt or to fight battles.

The Zhou Dynasty

One of the peoples who lived under Shang rule were the Zhou, who were based in the region around present-day Xi'an. About 1030 B.C. the Zhou overthrew the Shang and established their power by making family members and other powerful lords the rulers of subject states. At its height, Zhou power extended to Mongolia in the north and beyond the Chang River valley in the south.

Giving land to members of the royal family and setting up a system that allowed these lords to become powerful weakened the dynasty's power. The last 240 years or so of the Zhou dynasty became known as the Warring States period (475–221 B.C.), as powerful families formed huge armies and fought each other for land.

This time of violence was also a time of change and of new ideas and inventions. Confucianism (*see* box opposite) and Taoism first developed at this time. Great discoveries were also made in the fields of mathematics, medicine, and astronomy.

Confucius and Confucianism

The great Chinese thinker Confucius (551–479 B.C.) was a poor government official who believed that he had a divine mission to bring peace to troubled, war-torn China. At the age of 50, he began to wander from province to province trying to promote his ideas among the country's warlords.

There was little new about the ideas of Confucius. They were largely traditional values emphasizing the importance of the family in creating a peaceful and happy society. These traditional ideas were known as the Way of Heaven. At the heart of the Way of Heaven was the virtue of *ren*, meaning "goodness" or "kindness." In practice *ren* involves people showing respect and politeness to one another. One famous saying of Confucius was "Do not make others do what you would not want have done to you"—similar to the Golden Rule.

Central to Confucius's thinking was the problem of how to create a stable society. The warlords wanted to rule society by force of arms. Confucius argued that this solution was self-defeating: war and violence created only more war and violence. He blamed China's troubles on its bad rulers. Wicked kings and warlords corrupted the whole of society and brought down the anger of heaven. War, rebellion, and natural disasters such as earthquakes were the inevitable result of poor leadership, he believed. The Chinese call this idea the Mandate of Heaven. People who are poorly ruled have a right—even a duty—to rebel against their rulers.

Toward the end of his life, Confucius returned to his home in what is now Shandong province. There he edited classical Chinese works of literature and attracted a small band of followers. His ideas were not widely accepted during his lifetime, but later they became part of the official teachings of the Chinese administration. A collection of sayings by Confucius, called the *Analects*, became a textbook that all officials had to study, and his ideas spread throughout society. Even today many Chinese are able to quote some of Confucius's wise sayings. Notions about respect, politeness, and duty, and about the relationship between good government and a peaceful society, are still important to Chinese people today.

QIN AND HAN EMPIRES

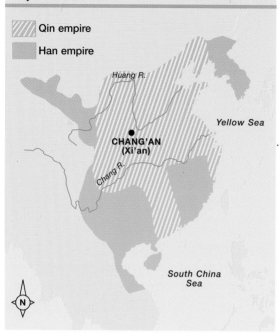

Qin empire

Han empire

Huang R.

Yellow Sea

CHANG'AN
(Xi'an)

Chang R.

South China Sea

N

This map shows the first great Chinese empires—those of the Qin (221–207 B.C.) and Han (206 B.C.–A.D. 220). Both empires had their capital at or near Chang'an, the present-day Xi'an.

Right is the Chinese character for the Qin dynasty. The name "Qin," sometimes spelled Ch'in, gave its name to China.

THE FIRST EMPEROR

The most successful of the warring states was Qin, which lay in the west of what is now China. The king of this state was Zheng, the most powerful of the warlords. He overthrew the Zhou ruler and established the first Chinese imperial dynasty. Zheng changed his title to Qin Shihuangdi, which means "first emperor of Qin."

Qin Shihuangdi unified China for the first time. He destroyed the rule of the aristocratic families, abolished the local states, and set up provinces with leaders answerable only to him. To help him rule his mighty empire, Shihuangdi organized a huge army of officials who made sure the emperor's laws were carried out.

The Rule of Law

The emperor based his new state on a philosophy called legalism. Unlike Confucianism, which argued that humans were naturally good and needed only a ruler to set them a good example, the idea of legalism was that people were bad and needed strict laws to keep them in order. Qin Shihuangdi started to unify his empire under a single set of laws and regulations. He standardized weights and measures and introduced a new standard coinage—a round copper coin with a square hole in it. He attempted to impose a single Chinese language and abolished regional variations in forms of writing.

At first sight one of Qin Shihuangdi's decrees seems very strange. He ordered that all carts should have

axles of the same length. At this time roads were not well surfaced and carts wore deep ruts in the road. Axle lengths varied from one area to another, so when carts moved from place to place the wheels did not always fit into the ruts. This made cart journeys long, hard, and even dangerous.

The emperor's idea was that if all axle lengths were the same, hauling carts would become easier, safer, and quicker. This kind of improvement was essential in a large empire, where grain sometimes had to be transported over long distances to feed large populations.

"Wherever the sun and moon shine, wherever people go by boat and carriage, men obey his orders..." **Qin-dynasty stone tablet.**

Strengthening the Empire

Qin Shihuangdi ruled his empire with an iron hand. At the cost of thousands of lives, he linked and extended the Great Wall that defended China from northern invaders (*see* p. 29). He tried to abolish free thought and ordered that all books of literature and philosophy be destroyed. This event, known as the Burning of the Books, was followed by the execution of more than 500 scholars whom the emperor regarded as opponents.

Qin Shihuangdi died in 210 B.C. and was buried in a huge tomb outside the imperial capital, Chang'an. The tomb was beautifully decorated and filled with rare and precious objects. It was guarded by crossbow traps, set to shoot anyone who tried to break in. Nearby an army of lifesize clay statues—the famous Terracotta Warriors—was buried (*see* p. 54).

Qin Shihuangdi, sitting in the pavilion at the top of the picture, orders the book-burning and the murder of scholars.

53

The Terracotta Warriors

In 1974 peasants digging a well close to the tomb of Qin Shihuangdi, near Xi'an, Shaanxi province, unearthed one of the world's great archaeological treasures—the Terracotta Warriors. Some 1,000 life-size and lifelike pottery soldiers were uncovered. Experts believe, however, that there may be as many as another 6,000 figures still buried.

For centuries before Qin Shihuangdi, powerful and wealthy rulers were buried in huge, palacelike tombs. Shihuangdi's tomb, however, was on a scale never seen before. At the beginning of his reign as king of Qin, Shihuangdi ordered some 700,000 men to begin work on the project. It was an astonishing feat of organization. Giant kilns (ovens) were fueled with tons of firewood to create the high temperatures necessary—about 1,800°F (980°C)—to harden the figures.

The emperor believed that the Terracotta Warriors would protect him in the afterlife. Even in his lifetime, the emperor lived in constant fear of assassination. He slept in a different place every night, and anyone who revealed his whereabouts was punished with death.

The soldiers are grouped in battle order, rank by rank, some mounted on horse-drawn chariots, others in infantry groups. The soldiers are armed with bronze spears, swords, and crossbows.

CHINA'S FIRST GOLDEN AGE

After Qin Shihuangdi's death, the empire was torn apart by civil war. Finally Liu Bang, a low-ranking official of the Qin government and leader of a rebel band, defeated the Qin army and proclaimed himself the first emperor of a new dynasty, the Han. Liu Bang (256–195 B.C.) took the name Gaodi, meaning "high emperor."

The Han ruled between 206 B.C. and A.D. 220. The 400-year dynasty was one of the longest-lasting in Chinese history. At its height its empire was bigger than that of imperial Rome, which flourished at about the same time. The Han presided over an era known as China's Golden Age. Art, education, and science thrived, and writers produced history books and dictionaries.

> The Han dynasty began to forge the Chinese national identity. The majority of Chinese people today still call themselves Han Chinese after this dynasty.

The Triumph of Confucianism

The Han dynasty was dominated by scholars who followed the philosophy of Confucius (*see* p. 51). The Confucians believed in a moral ruler, governing by the grace of heaven and maintaining the welfare of his subjects. At first Liu Bang was unconvinced by the Confucians. According to legend one of his advisors was in the habit of quoting from the *Books of Poetry and Documents*, a Confucian handbook. One day Liu Bang exclaimed in exasperation: "I won the empire on horseback. What use are the *Poetry and Documents*!" The advisor quietly pointed out that while an empire could be won by force, it could not be governed in the same way.

> "If any of the princes or governors discovers a man of talent and virtue under his jurisdiction, he should personally invite him to serve the government..." Decree by Gaodi.

One of the Confucians' measures was to set up a state administration, which brought stability to the country and helped to run China for the next 2,000 years. An imperial university was set up to teach Confucianism, and examinations selected "men of talent" as government officials. During the Han period, agriculture developed dramatically. Crop yields improved as the use of the ox-drawn plow, iron tools, and irrigation spread throughout the countryside.

This is the Chinese character for the Han dynasty (206 B.C.–A.D. 220).

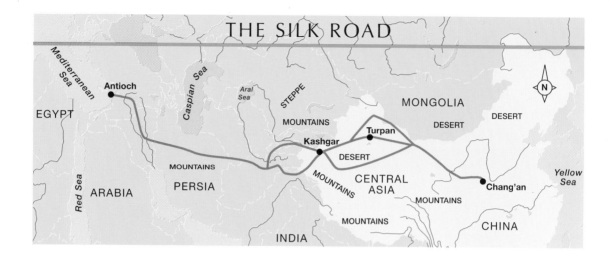

THE SILK ROAD

There were many "silk roads" between China and Europe. The main one stretched from Chang'an to the Mediterranean port of Antioch and onward to Rome. The route was long and difficult, passing between mountains and skirting deserts. Along the route were Buddhist holy places, such as the Bezeklik Thousand Buddha Caves, near Turpan, Xinjiang province (below).

The Han also expanded their territory and trade in all directions, far beyond the traditional Chinese borders. One famous trade route was the Silk Road across Central Asia. Traders went along this route to sell silk as far away as Rome and brought back heavier, stronger horses for China's imperial cavalry in addition to precious stones, perfume, pearls, and linen. Wandering Buddhist monks joined the trading caravans in order to travel safely into China. They preached to the people and founded monasteries along the route.

Rebellion and Disunity

Political struggles and corruption among royal court administrators disrupted the last century of Han rule. Powerful regional officials began ignoring the central government. A large-scale rebellion split China into three competing kingdoms: Wei, Shu, and Wu.

After the fall of the Han dynasty, these major kingdoms struggled for dominance and warred with each other almost continuously. In the north was the kingdom of Wei, which stretched south from the Great Wall to the Chang River; in the southeast was the kingdom of Wu; and in the Sichuan Basin was the state of Shu.

Paper and Printing

The ancient Chinese were clever inventors. Many of their ideas remained unknown in Europe until many centuries later, and some European "inventions" can even be traced back to a Chinese prototype. For example, the stirrup for horseriding appeared in China as long ago as the second century B.C. but took another 1,000 years to reach Europe. The wheelbarrow was used by the Chinese in the third century A.D. but was unknown in Europe until the 13th century. Other Chinese inventions were matches, the crossbow, and cast iron.

One of China's most brilliant and influential inventions was paper. The first recorded use of paper was at the Han court about A.D. 105. An official named Cai Lun created a sheet of paper using bark from the mulberry tree, fiber from the hemp plant, and old rags. Later the Chinese were able to make very beautiful papers that were fine, strong, and durable, providing a perfect surface for writing the elegant Chinese script. The Ming-dynasty picture below shows a a man using a bamboo screen to sift the paper fibers from the wood-pulp "soup."

The art of papermaking spread to other parts of the world only very slowly. Paper was manufactured in Baghdad in 793, and from there it spread to Europe.

Another area in which China led the world was printing. According to one story, the idea originated with Buddhist pilgrims who molded damp sheets of paper to the carved texts found on temple pillars and brushed the raised surface with ink to get copies of the texts.

This idea led to the development of wood-block printing in about the sixth century A.D. A text was written on a sheet of paper and, while the ink was still wet, the paper was applied to a smooth block of wood to leave an inky image. A wood carver cut away the areas not covered in ink so that the text stood out in relief and in reverse.

Next this wood block of "backward" writing was inked and a sheet of paper laid across it. The printer lightly rubbed the back of the paper with a brush, leaving an imprint of the text on the other side of the paper—this time the print appeared correct.

蕩料入簾

MEDIEVAL CHINA

Eventually one general, Yang Jian (541–604), was able to take control of northern China, and in 581 he established the Sui dynasty. He conquered the south, and China was united again after more than three centuries of disunity. Yang's title was Wendi ("Literary Emperor").

The Sui dynasty lasted a shorter period than many dynasties—from 581 to 618. Nevertheless the Sui emperors carried out some brilliant projects. They had the Great Wall rebuilt and had a series of connected waterways constructed that later became the basis for the Grand Canal (*see* p. 91). Around 5.5 million men were forced to work on these two projects. In some areas every commoner between the ages of 15 and 50 was forced to work.

The brutality of the Sui dynasty caused the people to rebel. This, combined with costly and unsuccessful wars against the nomadic Turks, led to the overthrow of Sui rule. A new dynasty, the Tang, was set up in its place.

This is the Chinese character for the Tang dynasty (A.D. 618–907). The first Tang emperor, Gaozu, named the new dynasty after the region of which he had previously been duke.

This 18th-century watercolor shows the powerful empress Wu Zetian.

The Tang Dynasty

Under the energetic Tang emperors, China enjoyed another "golden age" of prosperity, stability, and cultural flowering. Its armies triumphed over the "barbarians" who threatened the country's northern borders and extended China's influence deep into Central Asia. There was massive economic expansion, too. People started to use paper money, and a new banking system was introduced that allowed traders to deposit money. It was during this period that Buddhism reached its height of popularity (*see* box opposite).

One of the greatest Tang patrons of Buddhism was China's first reigning empress, Wu Zetian (624–705). Wu Zetian was a brilliant but ruthless

Buddhism Comes to China

The religion called Buddhism first developed in Nepal—the home of its founder Siddhartha Gautama (c. 563–483 B.C.). Siddhartha was a wealthy prince who was sickened by the poverty and suffering he found around him. He believed that human beings could never find happiness in the physical world and that all desires—love, hunger, thirst, and ambition—caused only misery.

Fulfillment, Siddhartha said, could be found only by overcoming such desires and by attaining *nirvana*, a state of complete freedom and enlightenment. Siddhartha became the first Buddha, which means "the enlightened one," and his ideas spread across Asia, carried by traveling monks.

Buddhism first reached China during the Han dynasty (206 B.C.–A.D. 220). The Han emperor Mingdi (A.D. 28–75) sent a mission to India to bring back Buddhist scriptures, called *sutras*. It was under the Tang, however, that Buddhism was widely adopted in China.

During the reign of the second Tang emperor, Taizong, a Buddhist pilgrim Xuan Zang (602–664) journeyed westward to India. His journey lasted 18 years, during which time he wandered around India collecting *sutras*. Taizong paid for the translation of many *sutras* into Chinese from Sanskrit, an ancient Indian language. Temples and monasteries were erected, and the government exempted these places from paying tax.

ruler. Once she became empress, she is said to have poisoned many of her close relatives to prevent them from threatening her power.

The capital, Chang'an, attracted diplomats, poets, and scholars from all over Asia and even Europe. Visitors included Buddhist priests from India, traders from Arabia, and travelers from Persia, Korea, and Japan. Traders made their way to Chang'an along the Silk Road or by ship to the southern port of Nanhai (later Guangzhou).

The last years of the Tang dynasty were marked by rebellion. The Tibetans seized control of China's western territories, blocking the Silk Road. In 879 a revolt broke out in Guangzhou, interrupting China's prosperous sea trade. The country was in chaos. In the general mood of mistrust of anything foreign, Chinese Buddhism suffered a decline from which it never recovered.

At the height of the Tang dynasty about A.D. 700, Chang'an was one of the greatest cities in the world. It spread over 30 square miles (78 sq. km) and had a population of more than one million people.

This is the character for the Song dynasty (960–1279). On the opposite page is the character for the Yuan dynasty (1279–1368).

The Song Dynasty

After the collapse of the Tang dynasty, China endured another period of disintegration, known as the Five Dynasties and the Ten Kingdoms. Between 907 and 960, there were five short-lived military dictatorships. Parts of northern China fell under foreign rule, while the south was divided into small states.

The ideal of a strong Chinese empire remained alive, however. In 960 a new dynasty emerged, the Song, which was able to push back the foreign invaders and reunite the fragmented country. The first Song emperor, Taizu (927–976), made the ancient city of Kaifeng the capital.

Unlike the emperors of the Tang dynasty who had tried to keep their empire together by fighting foreign wars, the tolerant and humane Song emperors concentrated on building up a strong administration. They encouraged the study of Confucianism once again, and learning and education were promoted over warfare.

TANG AND SONG EMPIRES

Yan (Beijing)

Huang R.

KAIFENG

Yellow Sea

CHANG'AN (Xi'an)
Luoyang

Chengdu

Chang R.

Nanhai (Guangzhou)

South China Sea

Tang empire

Song empire

Under the warlike Tang emperors (618–907), China once again expanded to much the same size as it had been under the Han dynasty. The Song empire (960–1279), though smaller, was maintained by politics rather than war.

The Song dynasty was an era of great achievements in art, poetry, and technology. Advances in mapmaking, mathematics, engineering, and astronomy created a kind of social revolution in China. There were new and better bridges, broad canals, and mighty ships, whose sails, one poet wrote, were like "great clouds in the sky." The invention of the compass helped the Chinese to become accomplished sailors.

With its huge, bustling cities, impressive engineering projects, and flourishing trade in luxury goods such as porcelain, silk, and jade, China was the most advanced nation of the world at that time.

MONGOL RULE

The Chinese had worried for centuries about the threat on their northern border. In 1206 the Mongol leader Temujin (about 1162–1227) took the title Genghis Khan, meaning "Universal Ruler," and led his army southward on a mission of conquest. For the first time, China fell under foreign rule, becoming part of a vast Mongol empire (*see* map below).

In 1279 Genghis Khan's grandson Kublai Khan (1215–1294) finally overthrew the remnants of the Song empire in the south of China. In its place he set up a Mongol dynasty of emperors, the Yuan, which ruled China for almost a century. China's Mongol rulers controlled the entire length of the Silk Road and reestablished trade between east and west. Foreigners began arriving in China, including the Venetian trader Marco Polo (1254–1324; *see* p. 62).

This silk painting shows Genghis Khan, the founder of the Mongolian empire, out hunting. At its height the empire stretched from the Pacific Ocean to the borders of Hungary in Europe.

It was under Mongol rule that Beijing first became important. It was established as the Khans' winter capital. The Mongols called it Khanbaliq. According to Polo the city had huge walls that formed a square of 6 miles (10 km) on each side.

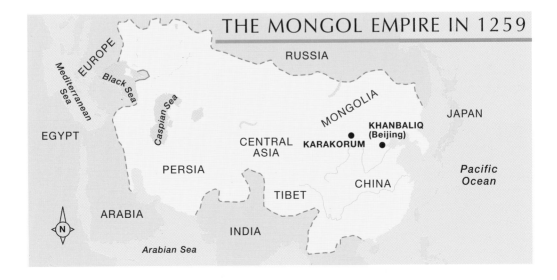

THE MONGOL EMPIRE IN 1259

RUSSIA

EUROPE

Mediterranean Sea

Black Sea

Caspian Sea

MONGOLIA

JAPAN

KHANBALIQ (Beijing)

CENTRAL ASIA

KARAKORUM

EGYPT

PERSIA

CHINA

Pacific Ocean

TIBET

ARABIA

INDIA

Arabian Sea

N

Silk, Spaghetti, and Ice Cream!

According to the book Venetian trader Marco Polo (1254–1324) wrote after his journeys, Polo went east from Europe with his father and his uncle to bring back silks to sell in Venice.

In 1263 the Polos were among the first Europeans to visit China, staying at the court of the Mongol emperor Kublai Khan. On a second journey to China in 1275, Marco Polo became a government official in the Mongol administration for 17 years. Kublai Khan did not want the Polos to leave, but the Polos finally arrived back in Venice in 1295. In addition to silk and porcelain, Marco Polo is also said to have brought back noodles and ice cream from China. Long, thin noodles later became known as spaghetti in Europe.

Some scholars argue that Marco Polo never went to China and just made up his book from what other people had written. Although his descriptions of China are sometimes surprisingly accurate, his book does not mention the Great Wall at all!

Genghis Khan's successors failed to maintain the unity of the Mongolian tribes, and the Mongol empire began to crumble. Throughout China rebel groups, such as the Red Turbans, plotted against the Yuan emperors. In the south, peasant leader Zhou Yuanzhang (1328–1398) founded a rival Chinese state with its capital at Nanjing on the Chang River. By 1368 Zhou Yuanzhang had driven the Mongols from China, recapturing Beijing and burning the old Mongol capital of Karakorum to the ground.

THE MING DYNASTY

Zhou Yuanzhang called his new dynasty Ming and set out to restore the glories of Tang and Song China. Lasting from 1368 to 1644, the Ming emperors strengthened the Great Wall and conquered the restless Mongolian peoples beyond. Manchuria, an area to the northeast, was occupied for the first time. In 1421 Beijing once again became the capital of China.

The Ming were also skilled diplomats. They attempted to establish relations with other countries and to increase China's political influence by

THE VOYAGES TO THE WEST

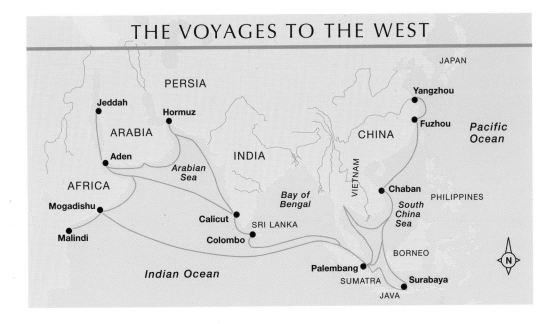

JAPAN

PERSIA

Jeddah

Hormuz

Yangzhou

ARABIA

Fuzhou

Pacific Ocean

CHINA

Aden

INDIA

Arabian Sea

AFRICA

VIETNAM

Mogadishu

Bay of Bengal

Chaban

PHILIPPINES

Calicut

SRI LANKA

South China Sea

Malindi

Colombo

BORNEO

N

Indian Ocean

Palembang

SUMATRA

Surabaya

JAVA

sending their officials overseas as ambassadors. Fifty years before Christopher Columbus sailed to the Americas, the Chinese admiral Zhang He (1371–1435) voyaged thousands of miles to southern India and as far as the east coast of Africa. He visited more than 30 countries and drew promises of allegiance to the emperor from their rulers.

Zhang took with him a fleet of large ships called junks, each of which could hold 1,000 men. The junks brought home many exotic goods to the Ming court, including rare spices, exotic plants, and curious animals such as zebras and giraffes.

From 1405 the Chinese admiral Zhang He led a series of great maritime expeditions. The early expeditions reached Java, Sri Lanka, and India, while later ones reached as far as Mogadishu and Malindi in East Africa and the Arabian ports of Aden and Jeddah.

The Europeans Reach China

European ships, too, were exploring the seas. The Portuguese began to explore the Chinese coast and to trade with the local people from about 1511. From 1557 Macau in southern China became a Portuguese colony. Catholic priests from the Jesuit order also came from Europe and tried to convert the Chinese to Christianity. Matteo Ricci (1552–1610) was a Jesuit, who had learned Chinese and

The Chinese character for the Ming dynasty (1368–1644) means "bright" or "brilliant."

studied the philosophy and customs of the country before he arrived. Ricci was also a brilliant astronomer and scientist and used his scientific skill to win the confidence of the emperor in Beijing. He produced the first Chinese map of the world, placing China at the center. Ricci converted many high-ranking Chinese men and women to Christianity and founded the first Christian mission in Beijing.

The Ming in Decline

In the 17th century, the Ming declined. The court in Beijing's Forbidden City was corrupt and extravagant. Landowners often lived in the cities and wasted their money on luxurious living. Taxes were very high to support the huge administration, and some poor families even had to sell their children to pay their taxes.

"I have offended ...against Heaven; the rebels have seized my capital because my ministers deceived me. Ashamed to face my ancestors, I die..." Chongzhen's suicide note.

There was also trouble on China's northern borders. The Manchus, a warrior people from the Mongolian grasslands, frequently made raids into China. Angry at the court corruption, an army of peasant rebels marched on Beijing in 1644 to overthrow the last Ming emperor, Chongzhen. As the army reached the capital, the emperor, full of self-reproach, slaughtered his wives and hanged himself from a tree in a park just outside the Forbidden City.

THE QING DYNASTY

The Manchus now seized the opportunity to cross the Great Wall and march south. They claimed that they were coming to help the Ming, but instead they put their own emperor—a six-year-old boy—on the throne. This was the beginning of the Qing dynasty, and once again China was under foreign rule.

The Manchurian dynasty of emperors called itself Qing, meaning "pure" or "clear."

The Qing emperors and the tiny Manchu minority who settled in China lived in constant fear of revolt. The Qing managed to keep power with a highly skilled and disciplined army and by continuing many of the traditions and policies of the Ming.

Despite this, the Qing were often highhanded in their relations with their Chinese subjects. For example, one imperial decree insisted that all Chinese men must wear their hair in a pigtail in the Manchu fashion. This was very unpopular, and a Chinese rebel's first act of defiance against Qing rule was often to cut off his pigtail.

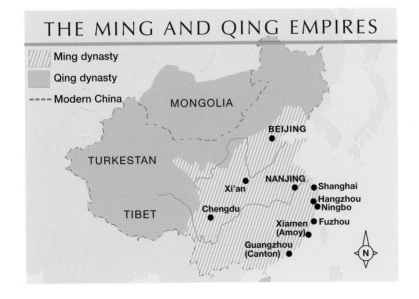

THE MING AND QING EMPIRES

Ming dynasty
Qing dynasty
Modern China

MONGOLIA
BEIJING
TURKESTAN
Xi'an NANJING
Shanghai
Hangzhou
Ningbo
Chengdu
TIBET
Xiamen Fuzhou
(Amoy)
Guangzhou
(Canton)
N

Under the Ming dynasty, China regained much of the ancient territories it had possessed under the Han and Tang. The Qing dynasty (1644–1911) extended the Chinese empire still farther, taking control of Tibet, Mongolia, and Turkestan.

Eventually, however, the Manchurian emperors became deeply influenced by Chinese culture. Kangsi (1654–1722) was one of the greatest of China's emperors. He reigned for 61 years, making him China's

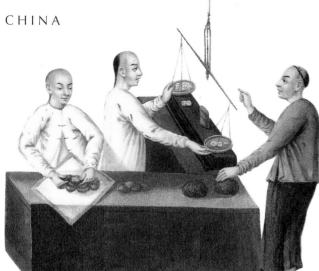

This 19th-century Chinese watercolor shows men weighing and selling opium in a shop. The port of Guangzhou, called Canton by the Europeans, was an important center for the opium trade.

The British seemed to be unaware of the immorality of the opium trade. One Sunday in 1839, a British captain wrote in his diary: "Employed delivering opium briskly. No time to read my Bible."

longest-reigning emperor. He loved Chinese literature and set up artists' work-shops in the Forbidden City. He also issued Confucian laws that stressed the virtue of obedience.

Tea and Opium

During the first 150 years of Manchu rule, the economy prospered and the borders of the empire expanded. New crops such as tobacco and corn were introduced. More and more Spanish, Portuguese, Dutch, and British traders arrived on China's coasts. They came to buy tea (*see* box opposite), spices, raw silk, and sugar, as well as manufactured goods such as porcelain.

The emperors were suspicious of the Europeans, whose greedy conquest of other parts of the world was well known. They tried to restrict the contacts that the new-comers had with the Chinese empire, and foreigners were permitted to trade only through the port of Guangzhou.

The Europeans, for their part, disliked the restrictions placed upon them, and their officials refused to kow-tow, or bow deeply to the emperor. Britain, the leading trading power of the 18th century, led the way in trying to force China to grant freer and cheaper trading conditions and to open more Chinese ports to British ships.

However, there was an imbalance in trade between China and Britain. British purchases of silk, tea, and porcelain were far greater than Chinese purchases of wool and spices. In addition, the British East India Company, one of the companies trading with China, did not want to pay in silver for Chinese goods. Instead the company grew opium poppies in India and processed them to extract opium, an addictive drug. They smuggled the opium into China in exchange for Chinese goods.

Opium-smoking first became popular in China during the 17th century, and many people became addicted to the drug. The emperors tried to ban its use, but prohibition had little effect because so many imperial officials smoked the drug. The British exploited the fashion and became the main dealers in opium. By 1800 as many as 400,000 chests of opium, each weighing 110 pounds (50 kg), had been sent to China.

In 1839, in a bid to stop the trade, China seized more than 20,000 chests of Indian opium and burned them. The British responded by blockading the port of Guangzhou and sinking several Chinese war junks. The Opium War had begun.

Britain quickly occupied some of China's important ports and forced a humiliating peace treaty on the emperor. Under the Treaty of Nanjing of 1842, China gave Britain the island of Hong Kong (*see* p. 44) as well as trading rights in five major ports: Guangzhou (Canton), Xiamen (Amoy), Fuzhou, Ningbo, and Shanghai. This was the first of what the Chinese called the "Unequal Treaties."

THE END OF IMPERIAL CHINA

The Europeans now divided China into "spheres of influence"—that is, areas in which each country was the controlling power. France took control of those southwestern areas that bordered its empire in Indochina; the British controlled the Chang River and the port of Shanghai; while the Germans controlled Shandong province. The Europeans treated a once-proud nation almost like a colony.

"All the Tea in China"

The ancient Chinese believed that tea could enable a person to live forever. At first they chewed the tea, which was compressed into cakes of tea leaves. Around A.D. 1000 the Chinese began to make a drink by pouring hot water on dried tea leaves and stirring it with a bamboo stick.

The first book in the world on tea was written by the poet Lu Yu (A.D. 733–804) during the Tang dynasty. According to legend Lu Yu became a god after his death and was revered by Chinese tea merchants everywhere.

Until the mid-17th century, tea was unknown in Europe. In the 18th century, tea-drinking became popular there, particularly in England. Fast sailing ships called tea clippers raced from Europe to China and back again so the freshest teas could be sold in Europe. By 1800 Britain had imported 23 million pounds (10.4 million kg) of tea. Britain was so famous for drinking tea that one Chinese official believed that the British could not survive unless they drank tea.

> "Vast columns of smoke were seen rising to the northwest...The barbarians had entered the Summer Palace and...set fire to the buildings. Their excuse for this abominable behavior is that their troops got out of hand."
> A letter written by an inhabitant of Beijing during the 1860 occupation.

The humiliation was too much for many Chinese people. In 1851 a Christian fanatic named Hong Xiuquan (1814–1864) led a massive revolt against Qing rule in Guangxi province. In the Tai Ping ("great peace") Rebellion, 10,000 rebels rampaged through the countryside and seized the city of Nanjing. Hong was proclaimed "Heavenly King," and Nanjing became the "Heavenly Kingdom of Great Peace." The revolt, which lasted until 1864, caused widespread destruction. Some 20 million people died during the rebellion.

In 1858 a second war between Britain and China, known as the Arrow War, or the Second Opium War, broke out. Britain allied with France, and in 1860 their troops occupied Beijing and set fire to the city's Imperial Summer Palace. Defeated once again, the Chinese were forced to make even more trade concessions to the West. Eleven more ports were opened to the Russians, Germans, and Japanese, as well as to the French and the British. The Portuguese formally took over the port of Macau in 1887.

The Boxer Rebellion

In 1900 there was an uprising called the Boxer Rebellion aimed at driving foreigners out of northern China. The Boxers got their name because they practiced a form of Chinese martial art and belonged to a society called the "Righteous and Harmonious Fists." They attacked Christian missionaries and burned down churches. They tore down telegraph lines and blew up railroads because they saw them as "foreign."

The Boxers won favor from China's dowager empress Ci Xi (1835–1908). Ci Xi had imprisoned her son, the emperor Guang-xu, in the rebuilt Summer Palace

A Chinese woodblock print shows the Boxer rebels taking a city.

and ruled in his name. She credited the Boxers with magical powers and believed they could help her rid China of Western influence.

With Ci Xi's approval, the Boxers entered Beijing and besieged the foreign quarter. In one episode French and Italian sailors defended some 4,000 Chinese Christians who had sought refuge in the Catholic cathedral. The Western countries, including the United States, sent 20,000 soldiers to end the siege. Ci Xi and the emperor fled the capital disguised as peasants.

The Western forces let Ci Xi return to Beijing on the condition that she reform Chinese society. In 1908, however, the empress died. Guang-xu was murdered on Ci Xi's orders just before her own death. His three-year-old nephew, Pu Yi (1905–1967), became ruler.

Republican Revolution

Many Chinese people associated the rule of the emperors with the hated Manchu minority. They believed that imperial rule should be replaced by a republic. In this way, they believed, China could finally be rid of foreign rule and return to its roots.

The Last Emperor

China's last emperor, Pu Yi, was three years old when he ascended the throne. He reigned for just four years. After the end of imperial rule in 1911, Pu Yi was allowed to continue to live in the Imperial City, with a pension of some four million dollars a year.

Pu Yi was destined to spend his life as a political pawn. In 1924 a warlord expelled him from the palace, and he took refuge with the Japanese. In 1934 the Japanese gave him the title of emperor of Manchuria as a way of making their occupation of the region seem legitimate (legal) (see p. 71). Under the Chinese communist government, Pu Yi was "re-educated," and until the end of his life in 1967, he worked contentedly as a gardener.

The most important republican leader was Sun Yat-sen (1866–1925), who lived in exile in the West, Japan, Hawaii, and Hong Kong. In 1911 Sichuan province declared itself independent. Fourteen other provinces followed suit, and Sun Yat-sen returned to China to become the president of a new republic based in the southern city of Nanjing. The Manchu leaders finally agreed to the abdication of the young emperor.

NATIONALISTS AND COMMUNISTS

The new Chinese republic was far from united. Powerful warlords ruled their own areas, and various groups struggled to impose overall control. In 1912 Sun Yat-sen formed the nationalist party, the Kuomintang (KMT), which aimed to reunite China. After Sun Yat-sen's death in 1925, his brother-in-law, Chiang Kai-shek (1887–1975), took over the party leadership.

Meanwhile, in Shanghai, a small group of people set up the Chinese Communist Party (CCP). Among its youthful, idealistic leaders was a university librarian named Mao Zedong (1893–1976). The new party was supported by the communist government of Russia, which advised the CCP leaders to join forces with the KMT and finally rid China of the warlords.

In 1926 the combined forces of the nationalists and communists swept through China under the leadership of Chiang. The campaign, known as the Northern Expedition, successfully rooted out some warlords, but the alliance soon fell apart. In 1927 the communists seized Shanghai and organized a general strike against Chiang. Chiang retaliated by ordering a massacre of the communists. Some 5,000 people died in the massacre, including Mao's young wife, Yang Kaihui.

The Long March

In October 1928, Chiang Kai-shek set up a national government and declared himself president. Chiang brutally oppressed all opposition to his regime, and relied on the support of big business and Western countries such as Great Britain to hold on to power. There was widespread corruption, and Chiang did little to lessen the poverty of the Chinese people.

The communists withdrew to China's remoter regions, particularly the southern province of Jiangxi, where Mao Zedong set up a stronghold in the Jingang Mountains. Even there, however, the communists came under attack from the nationalists, and in 1934 Chiang

Unlike the nationalist forces, who often looted, soldiers of the communist People's Liberation Army were told "Do not even take a needle or a thread. Consider the people as your family. All that you have borrowed you must return."

"The enemy advances, we retreat; the enemy camps, we harass; the enemy tires, we attack; the enemy retreats, we pursue." Red Army saying.

surrounded the Jingang Mountains with half a million troops. Mao Zedong now came up with a tactical masterstroke. On October 15, 1934, Mao set out on a desperate 6,000-mile (9,700 km) retreat from Jiangxi, called the Long March. With him went 85,000 soldiers and 15,000 party officials.

When the marchers arrived in their new base in Shaanxi province a year later, only 30,000 had survived. Nevertheless, the Long March saved the communist forces from being completely wiped out by the KMT, and the communists were able to continue their guerrilla warfare against the KMT.

THE LONG MARCH

Revolutionary bases 1934
Revolutionary base 1935
→ Route of Red Army

Beijing

SHANXI

Yellow Sea

NINGXIA

Yan'an

Huang R.

JIANGSU

GANSU   SHAANXI   HENAN

QINGHAI   HUBEI   ANHUI   Shanghai

ZHEJIANG

SICHUAN   Chang R.

JIANGXI

HUNAN   FUJIAN   Taiwan

GUIZHOU   Jingang Mountains

YUNNAN   GUANGDONG

GUANGXI

N   South China Sea

Invasion and Civil War

Japan had already seized the northern Chinese province of Manchuria in 1931–1932, and in July 1937, the Japanese launched a full-scale invasion of China. Chiang Kai-shek was intent on crushing the communist guerrillas and underestimated the strength of Japan's Imperial Army. By October 1938, the Japanese controlled all the eastern provinces. The government troops mutinied against Chiang and forced him to enter a new alliance with the communists to fight the Japanese. When World War II broke out in 1939, China fought on the side of the Allies.

After Japan's defeat in 1945, civil war broke out in China. On one side were the communists, backed by the Soviet Union, and, on the other, the nationalists, who received help from the United States. Using the guerrilla tactics improved against the Japanese, the communists gained control of most of northern China by 1948, and in 1949 they declared a new government. The nationalists fled to Taiwan, where they set up a rival government.

In October 1934, Mao Zedong ordered a massive retreat of the communist forces. During the Long March, 100,000 people trekked 6,000 miles (9,700 km) from the Jingang Mountains, on the Jiangxi–Hunan border, to communist-held Yan'an, Shaanxi province. On the way they crossed 11 provinces, 18 mountain ranges, and 24 rivers. Many thousands died of sickness, exposure, exhaustion, or the cold.

71

Chairman Mao

Chinese Communist leader Mao Zedong (1893–1976) is one of the towering figures of the 20th century. He was the eldest of four children, born into a prosperous farming family in Hunan province, in southwest China. At 16 he left home to study at a middle school in Changsha, where he read works on politics and economics as well as the Confucian classics. His heroes were the warrior emperors of Chinese history, such as Qin Shihuangdi, as well as Western leaders such as George Washington.

Mao was introduced to communist ideas while working in the library at Beijing University. Between 1921 and 1927, Mao organized peasant uprisings and strikes for workers in southern China. From 1931 Mao led a guerrilla war against the nationalist government in Jiangxi, and in 1935 he ordered the Long March (see p. 71). During this time, too, he became leader, or chairman, of the Chinese Communist Party.

Mao's moment of triumph came on October 1, 1949, when he proclaimed the People's Republic of China. Chairman Mao set out to transform China, adapting communist ideas to his country's particular needs. By liberating the peasants from the landlords, he believed, the whole of China could be freed.

Mao was not as good a nation-builder as he was a revolutionary. Many of his schemes brought chaos and cost the lives of tens of millions of people. In many ways Mao was not unlike some of the emperors who built the Chinese empire.

The death of Mao in 1976 stunned the Chinese people, who had been taught to worship him. Mao's collection of sayings, the "Little Red Book" was seen as a guide to life. Even today thousands of Chinese people visit his mausoleum in Beijing. Over the Gate of Heavenly Peace nearby, where Mao proclaimed the People's Republic in 1949, a huge portrait (above) still hangs of the "Great Helmsman."

THE PEOPLE'S REPUBLIC OF CHINA

On October 1, 1949, Mao Zedong stood with his comrades at the Gate of Heavenly Peace (*see* p. 36), the entrance to the Forbidden City, and proclaimed the People's Republic of China (PRC). "The Chinese people have stood up," he declared. China, however, was in great need of economic and social reform.

The communists were determined to build a great nation. They reasserted central control over the country, reorganizing the country into provinces and regions (*see* p. 18). In 1951 the Red Army reoccupied Tibet, which since 1911 had enjoyed independence. The communists banned private business and brought the economy under central control (*see* pp. 81–82). They took all land from the landlords and divided it among the peasants.

The takeover of the land was completed by December 1952, but almost immediately Mao introduced a new land reform. His idea was for peasants to pool tools, labor, animals, and land and to work together planting and harvesting. By the end of 1956, 96 percent of peasant households had been forced into large socialist communes, in which people farmed the land together in groups. Mao saw the communes as a replacement for the family. Everyone ate together, and childcare was provided by the commune.

The communists did not tolerate any hint of opposition. Party officials, in combination with some peasants seeking revenge, accused others of the "crime" of being landlords at public meetings. Many were shot in the head after a brief trial. Sometimes people who simply expressed opinions different from those of the Communist Party were punished in this way.

A Hundred Flowers and a Great Leap Forward

On May 1, 1957, Mao launched the Hundred Flowers Campaign. This short period of liberty was named after two lines from a classical poem: "Let a hundred flowers bloom, let a hundred schools of thought contend."

The communists used a whole series of new words for accusing others:
• capitalist-roader—someone who believed that capitalism was a good idea
• rightist—someone whose political ideas were not radical enough or not close enough to those of the Communist Party
• revisionist—someone who thought that the ideas of the Chinese Communist Party needed to be revised or changed.

Many thinkers seized the opportunity to criticize the Communist Party's hold on power and to call for freedom of thought in schools and universities. There was so much criticism that the leadership was worried, and Mao ordered a crackdown. In the period that followed, thousands of people were accused of being "rightists" and were exiled to the countryside to work in the fields.

In February 1958, Mao launched another scheme, the Great Leap Forward. This was an energetic attempt to boost China's industry. Mao boasted that China's industrial output would match that of the United States in 15 or 20 years.

The Great Leap Forward was a disaster. The high production targets that were set could be reached only by producing poor-quality goods. Industrialization also disrupted agriculture. The Beijing government ordered the peasant communes to produce huge quantities of steel. To meet the quotas, peasants had to stop working in the fields, and there was a slump in food production. Droughts and floods in 1959 made matters even worse. A famine followed, and some 30 million people died.

This communist print from 1951 shows the May Day Parade in Tiananmen Square, Beijing. Throughout the communist world—for example Cuba, Vietnam, and North Korea—May 1 is International Labor Day and a national public holiday.

Different Kinds of Communism

Mao's version of communism worried the communist Soviet Union because it seemed as if Mao was undermining its role as head of the communist world. In 1960 the Soviet Union cancelled its aid program to China. In 1969 there were clashes between the two countries at their common border. From that time almost until the collapse of the Soviet Union in 1991, the two communist giants remained hostile toward each other.

The Cultural Revolution

In May 1966, Mao launched another movement, called the Great Proletarian Cultural Revolution. It aimed to root out "revisionists" and "capitalists" in the Communist Party and at keeping the spirit of revolution alive.

The people who took up Mao's call became known as Red Guards. These enthusiastic young party members rose up throughout China, seizing universities and schools, and eventually taking control of entire cities. Above all, the Red Guards attacked the so-called "Four Olds:" old ideas, old culture, old customs, and old habits.

Teachers and officials were beaten to death, sent into exile in the countryside, or humiliated by Red Guards. Specialization and expertise or knowledge of foreign

The "bible" of the Red Guard was *Quotations from Chairman Mao*, which was nicknamed the "Little Red Book."

A "Capitalist-roader"

During the Cultural Revolution, the Red Guards controlled China's cities. They abused and sometimes tortured anyone suspected of not believing in Mao's ideas. In this excerpt from her book *Wild Swans*, Jung Chang (born 1952) recalls how Communist Party thugs attacked and humiliated her mother, who had been accused of being a "capitalist-roader."

At meetings held to denounce her, these ex-convicts were particularly active. One day she [Chang's mother] came home with her face twisted in pain. She had been ordered to kneel on broken glass. My grandmother spent the evening picking fragments of glass from her [Chang's mother's] knees with tweezers and a needle. The next day,

she made my mother a pair of thick kneepads. She also made her a padded waist protector, because the tender structure of the waist was where the assailants always aimed their punches.

Several times my mother was paraded through the streets with a dunce cap on her head, and a heavy placard hanging from her neck on which her name was written with a big cross over it to show her humiliation… Every few steps, she and her colleagues were forced to go down on their knees and kowtow to the crowds. Children would be jeering at her. Some would shout that their kowtowing did not make enough noise and demand that they do it again. My mother and her colleagues then had to bang their foreheads loudly on the stone pavement.

languages were viewed with suspicion. Objects or books from the West and treasures from China's imperial past were destroyed. Tibet's beautiful Buddhist temples were ransacked or damaged. Only the presence of the army prevented anarchy in the country.

At the beginning of the 1970s, Mao became very sick and was increasingly unable to govern the country. A veteran of the Long March named Zhou Enlai (1898–1976) steered Chinese politics along less radical lines during this period. He opened up diplomatic and trading contacts with the West, and in 1971 China became a member of the United Nations. In 1972 U.S. President Richard Nixon made an historic visit to China. America was deeply worried that China would overcome its differences with the Soviet Union and form a powerful communist pact.

China is one of the world's nuclear powers. It exploded its first atom bomb in 1964.

Deng Xiaoping and Modernization

Early in 1976 Zhou died. Four leading radicals in the Communist Party, known as the Gang of Four, briefly gained the upper hand. They saw themselves as Maoist and wanted a return to the policies of the Cultural Revolution. On September 9, Mao himself died. Waiting to take control was Deng Xiaoping (1904–1997).

During the Cultural Revolution, Deng had been forced into exile in the countryside by Mao, but was given back his official post in 1977. By 1979 Deng had become the most important politician in the country. With the help of people who had a more moderate and practical approach to government, Deng began to overhaul China's economy.

"Chinese history is about to turn a new page, Tiananmen Square is ours, the people's, and we will not allow the butchers [the Chinese army] to tread on it." Student protester, May 1989.

Deng's key program was called the "Four Modernizations," aimed at upgrading industry, agriculture, science and technology, and defense. He began to allow more private business. The reforms, however, were economic and not political. Chinese people still had no say in the government, and in May 1989 pro-democracy protests broke out in Tiananmen Square, Beijing.

The Tiananmen Square Massacre

By the late 1980s, China's economy was out of control. Inflation was rising, and many people took advantage of their official positions to get money for themselves. The income gap between workers and the more privileged social classes was widening. Discontent and the pro-democracy stirrings in Eastern Europe inspired a movement for greater freedom and an end to corruption.

In 1989 in Tiananmen Square, Beijing, students set up a Goddess of Democracy facing the huge portrait of Mao (*see* p. 72). This statue was 30 feet (9 m) high and was modeled on the Statue of Liberty in New York. The students were joined in their protest by many thousands of discontented workers.

The Chinese government brought troops into Beijing from all over the country, but for six weeks it let the student protest continue. On the night of June 4, however, the troops moved in, using tanks and machine-gun fire to clear the square and the nearby avenues. Students tried hopelessly to stop the advance of the tanks (*see* photo above).

No one knows exactly how many people were killed in the Tiananmen massacre. The government admitted that 23 students were killed, but human-rights groups estimate the number of deaths to be closer to 1,000. By July 17, some 4,600 protesters had been arrested. Countries around the world condemned the massacre.

After the Tiananmen Square Massacre (*see* p. 77), Deng carried out more reforms, partly to keep the people happy. Mao's radical ideas were left behind. Deng abolished collective farms and allowed farmers to sell their surplus produce at markets. He encouraged small shops and businesses, and parts of the country were transformed into industrial regions intended to create goods for export. Former Red Guards turned to capitalism and set up businesses. Deng said: "To get rich is glorious."

Under Deng, the traditional business skills of the Chinese people were revived. China's economy boomed. By the early 1990s, the standard of living of many Chinese people had improved dramatically.

The "Little Helmsman"

Deng Xiaoping can be called the creator of today's China and had the nickname of the "Little Helmsman." People who met Deng were struck by his small size—he was under 5 feet tall (1.5 m)—and by his chain-smoking, but especially by the hard look in his eye. Deng rejected extreme political ideas and was just interested in getting things done. After the Great Leap Forward, he famously said, "I do not care whether a cat is black or white as long as it catches mice."

Deng's Legacy

Deng died in February 1997 and left behind him a country in which free enterprise (a situation in which governments do not interfere with private business) was allowed and a fast-growing economy that has the potential to become the largest in the world (*see* pp. 81–91). He created a middle class for whom communist political ideas were no longer a prime motivation in life. For the first time in China's history, many more people could choose what they did for a living, what they ate, and what they bought—even if this was at the cost of a growing gap between the rich and poor.

On the other hand, Deng's "socialist market economy" did not allow China to move toward democracy. Critics of the government are persecuted or sent into exile, and freedom of speech is restricted. What China's political dissidents (critics) call the "Fifth Modernization"—liberty—remains out of reach.

CONSTITUTION AND ADMINISTRATION

The constitution of the People's Republic of China describes the country's system of government as "a democratic dictatorship." This means in theory that the people—the workers and the peasants—control the administration of the government. In practice it is the Chinese Communist Party (CCP) that holds absolute power—it claims to be the sole representative of the people.

Deng's successor, Jiang Zemin, became general secretary of the CCP—the highest office in the party—when he took over. Jiang also became China's president and commander-in-chief of the armed forces, the People's Liberation Army (PLA), when he came to power.

The CCP is based in the capital, Beijing. Almost every top civilian, police, and military position is held by a CCP member. Because many of China's provinces are very far from the capital, local officials usually have a lot of power in deciding how the party's policies are carried out.

This system is not so different from that of imperial China. There is no emperor, of course. Instead there is a committee made up of 22 leading members of the CCP. This powerful committee, called the Politburo, is even based in a part of the Forbidden City, and its workings can seem just as mysterious as those of the old imperial palace.

China does have a parliament, called the National People's Congress (NPC). However, only candidates approved by the CCP are elected to the NPC, and the congress meets only for two or three weeks a year to rubber-stamp laws and decisions made by the Politburo.

China's army, the People's Liberation Army (PLA), is one of the most powerful in the world. It has a personnel of some three million members, 8,000 large tanks, 52 submarines, and almost 5,000 combat aircraft.

The National People's Congress is housed in the Great Hall of the People, on the western side of Tiananmen Square. The building also has a 5,000-seat banquet room, where President Richard Nixon was entertained during his visit in 1972.

The Economy

"China is a sleeping giant. Let her lie and sleep, for when she awakens she will astonish the world."

French emperor Napoléon Bonaparte (1769–1821)

For hundreds of years, the Chinese economy relied overwhelmingly on agriculture. Millions of peasants worked hard in the rice fields to feed themselves and the minority of people who lived in China's cities. The peasants lived in fear of flood and famine, but generally China was self-sufficient—that is, it could feed itself.

Under communism China rapidly industrialized and the Beijing government took control of the entire economy. The cost of this transformation was enormous. There were devastating famines in the countryside as planting and harvesting were neglected, while in the factories, incompetent management meant that output was low.

In the 1980s the Chinese economy shifted again—this time toward free enterprise, though still within a communist system. Industry boomed. Some experts say that the country could challenge the United States and the European Union as an economic power as early as 2020.

FACT FILE

• China's communist government has run the economy as a succession of Five-Year Plans. The Ninth Five-Year Plan ran from 1996 to 2000.

• Today there are five million *renminbi* millionaires in China, many of whom live in the prosperous province of Guangdong.

• Since the early 1990s, China's economy has grown by an average of 12.3 percent per year.

• Despite massive improvements in China's railroad and highway systems and the rapid increase in automobile ownership, the most common form of travel is still the bicycle.

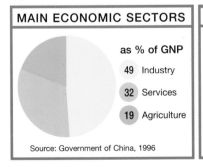

MAIN ECONOMIC SECTORS

as % of GNP

49 Industry

32 Services

19 Agriculture

Source: Government of China, 1996

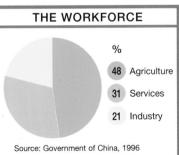

THE WORKFORCE

%

48 Agriculture

31 Services

21 Industry

Source: Government of China, 1996

In China every little bit of fertile land is used for crops. These rice terraces are in the mountainous province of Guizhou in China's southwest.

Between 1957 and 1978, China's annual grain production increased by only 2.6 percent, and the country had to import grain to feed its growing population.

A man in a bamboo hat plants rice in Guizhou province, southwest China. The cultivation of rice requires a lot of effort and can be back-breaking work.

THE IRON RICE BOWL

Before 1949 China was less developed than almost every other major nation. The vast majority of its people worked on the land, where they were at the mercy of unscrupulous landlords, devastating floods, and unpredictable weather. China's main industrial centers were Shanghai, Guangzhou, Nanjing, Tianjin, and Wuhan, which were linked by a poor rail and road network.

During the communist revolution, Mao and the other leaders inspired the peasants with a dream of a better life. They promised that China would become an "iron rice bowl," a guaranteed source of food that could never be taken away by greedy or cruel warlords, or broken by war or poor harvests.

Agriculture was the earliest focus of the communists. The country's economy hardly functioned, and a huge population had to be fed. Mao took the land from the landlords and divided it among 300 million peasants. The resulting strips of land were too small, however, to farm properly. Communal farming was also tried (*see* p. 73), but it was not very successful.

The Four Modernizations

After Mao died, a new leader, Deng Xiaoping, introduced the "Four Modernizations" program in 1978. Individuals were allowed to set up small shops and businesses. Families were also allowed to cultivate small patches of land for their own needs, although land ownership remained in the government's hands. Finally, all communal land ownership was ended. By 1984 all but 2 percent of farm households were handed back to families.

The PLA and Big Business

One of the biggest entrepreneurs in China is the armed forces. There are some three million people in the People's Liberation Army (PLA), and it controls a business empire with 20,000 enterprises, ranging from discos and restaurants to herbal medicine products.

These businesses are mostly small- and medium-sized, but altogether they provide around one-third of the military budget. The PLA started many of the businesses to finance military expenditure. For example, the main activity of one company was the production of military planes, but it had to go into making buses, jeeps, window frames, televisions, hovercraft, and many other products to raise money for building aircraft. Today the Chinese government wants to take over the PLA businesses, so that the army can concentrate on its military role.

The results were astonishing. By 1987, 50 percent more rice and wheat were produced than under the collectivized system. Cash income to farmers was four times greater. Huge amounts of high-quality food poured into the cities, and the standard of living of the peasants improved many times over.

Realizing that China could not develop by itself, Deng allowed some coastal provinces to accept foreign capital and to trade with less government control. The idea was to combine foreign money with China's huge, cheap pool of labor and generate prosperity that would spread to poorer regions.

In 1979 the government came up with the idea of the Special Economic Zone (SEZ). The SEZs offered tax breaks and a relaxation of labor regulations and employment conditions to foreign firms that set up factories in joint ownership with Chinese companies.

China was open for business. Money poured into the SEZs. Billions of U.S. dollars were invested in China. Overseas Chinese—mainly from Hong Kong, Taiwan, Singapore, and Malaysia—led the way. In addition to cash investment, these investors brought efficient management techniques, and up-to-date equipment.

China's Special Economic Zones (SEZs) are:
- Shenzhen, Guangdong
- Zhuhai, Guangdong
- Shantou, Guangdong
- Xiamen, Fujian
- the island of Hainan

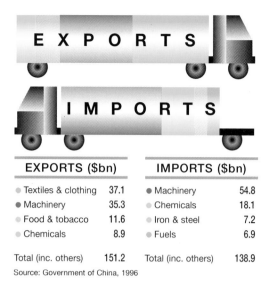

EXPORTS ($bn)		IMPORTS ($bn)	
Textiles & clothing	37.1	Machinery	54.8
Machinery	35.3	Chemicals	18.1
Food & tobacco	11.6	Iron & steel	7.2
Chemicals	8.9	Fuels	6.9
Total (inc. others)	151.2	Total (inc. others)	138.9

Source: Government of China, 1996

China's major trading partners are its near neighbors, Japan and Korea. Major exports include clothing and electronic goods.

MAIN TRADING PARTNERS

EXPORTS

%
21.8 Hong Kong
20.4 Japan
17.7 United States
5.0 South Korea
3.9 Germany
31.2 Others

IMPORTS

%
21.0 Japan
11.7 Taiwan
11.6 United States
9.0 South Korea
5.6 Hong Kong
41.1 Others

Source: Government of China, 1996

Tens of thousands of companies were started. Factories made shoes, clothes, textiles, toys, and household gadgets for export to Asia, Europe, and North America. By early 1981 China was a creditor nation (it was owed more by other countries than it owed abroad.)

When Hong Kong officially became part of the People's Republic again on July 1, 1997, China's economy had another boost. It gained a rich city with foreign currency reserves (stores of foreign money held by a central bank) that were the third largest in the world. Hong Kong also had one of the world's biggest economies, as well as 6.5 million citizens famous for their hard work and business skills.

Chinese people who were bright enough, worked hard, or had good business contacts rapidly became wealthy. By the end of 1997, the output of 29.5 million private companies, employing 68 million people, accounted for 11.3 percent of China's gross national product (GNP). The GNP is the total value of goods annually produced by one country. Private enterprise is now a major part of the economy. In September 1997, the government changed the status of privately owned businesses from a "supplemental" part to a "significant" part of the economy.

IMPORTS AND EXPORTS

By 1995 China was the seventh-largest economy in the world. Its main exports today are consumer goods, commodities, textile materials and clothes, oil, machinery and transportation equipment, gasoline, minerals, vegetables, and fruit. Although there is a large trading surplus (the value of the country's exports exceeds the value of its imports), China now imports much more than before. It needs to bring in technology and new equipment to help with modernizing its agriculture and industry and to produce consumer goods for people who now have more money to spend. Among the main goods imported to China today are telecommunications equipment, aircraft, automobiles, grain, books, paper, and metal.

China trades a lot with Japan mainly because the two countries are near each other and share many cultural traditions. The country exports almost as much to the United States but imports far fewer U.S. goods. The result is that China now has a trade surplus with the United States. This causes political friction because the U.S. government would prefer China buy more U.S. goods.

HOW CHINA USES ITS LAND

- Cropland
- Forest
- Pasture
- High mountains
- Desert

China's cropland is concentrated on the great flood plains in the eastern part of the country. The highlands in the western part of the country are rich in pastureland. The chart below shows land use as a percentage of the total productive land.

MAJOR SECTORS

One of the most important jobs of the Chinese economy is to feed the country's huge population. Agriculture therefore remains the backbone of the Chinese economy. A reliable supply of rice and other foods is essential if China is to avoid the devastating famines of the past.

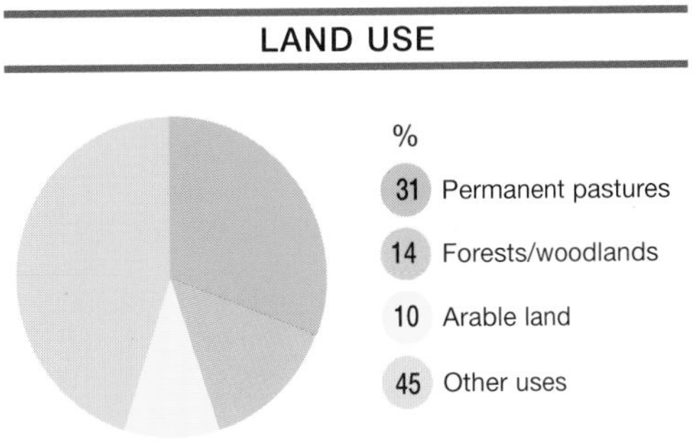

LAND USE

%
- 31 Permanent pastures
- 14 Forests/woodlands
- 10 Arable land
- 45 Other uses

Source: Government of China

85

China is one of the world's largest steel producers. In 1997 the country produced 29.4 million tons (26.77 million t).

Most of China's industry is concentrated in the eastern part of the country, close to transportation links and the ports.

Agriculture and Industry

Unlike most major countries in the world, agriculture and fishing are still a very important sector in China. They account for 19 percent of the GNP and employ 48 percent of the labor force. Agricultural exports such as food make up one-fifth of China's total exports. China is among the world's largest producers of rice, potatoes, peanuts, and tea (*see* p. 67). Commercial crops include cotton and other fibers and oilseeds.

In the industrial sector, two heavy industries—steelmaking and shipbuilding—remain important but are in need of reform. Like many national enterprises, these industries have large debts, too many workers, and management styles that date back to Mao's time.

Manufacturing is the brightest spot in the economy. This sector employs a quarter of China's labor force, and the country is the world's largest manufacturer of footwear and toys. China is working hard to improve the

MAJOR INDUSTRIES

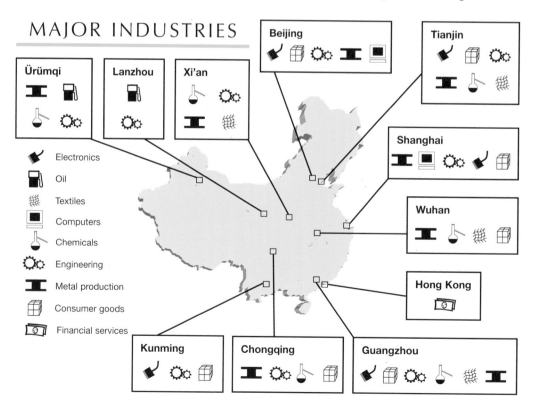

Employees stand next to a conveyor belt as they check the final detail on sneakers.

technological skills of its people, especially in computer and software manufacturing. Today there is a generation of software programmers in China who are widely respected for their inventiveness.

China has no major aircraft manufacturer, but it has had a space program since 1970. It has the capacity to make satellites and launch them on its "Long March" rockets from sites in Shanxi and Sichuan provinces.

Energy: From Coal to Hydroelectricity

Coal provides three-quarters of China's energy. Since the coal reserves are vast, estimated at 990 billion tons (900 billion t), coal will be the country's main energy source for some time. Annual coal production doubled between 1977 and 1992 to 1.21 billion tons (1.1 billion t). However, this was still not enough to meet China's needs.

One disadvantage of using so much coal is that when it is burned in power stations and factories to produce electricity, the low-grade quality of the coal causes a lot of pollution. China is looking for other sources to generate electricity. It wants to harness the power of its rivers and develop more hydroelectric power. There are already three nuclear power plants in China, and more are planned.

ENERGY SOURCES

%

82 Oil, gas, coal, and diesel

18 Hydroelectricity

Source: Government of China

On average a Chinese person uses 650 watts of electricity each year. In the United States, the average is 11,000 watts per person.

China's numerous and powerful rivers are a valuable source of energy. Their water is stored by dams and reservoirs and used to drive water turbines and generators, which produce electricity. The Linjiaxia Dam, seen here, blocks the Huang River as it flows through the Linjiaxia Gorge near Lanzhou.

Electricity supplies are not evenly distributed throughout the country. There are still 100 million people in China who do not have electricity, especially in provinces such as Gansu, Qinghai, Henan, and Sichuan. In some areas on the coast, there is electricity to spare.

Average crude-oil production of 184 million tons (167 million t) a year makes China the sixth-largest oil producer in the world. Ninety-five percent of the country's oil reserves are underground. Around 40 percent of China's total oil production comes from the Daqing Oilfield in the northeastern province of Heilongjiang.

The Three Gorges Dam

For centuries China's leaders have dreamed of taming the Chang River, which each summer claims the lives of many people when it floods. Engineers are now hard at work at the Three Gorges, building what will be the the world's largest hydroelectric dam. The idea is to try to control the flooding and to generate electricity for homes and factories. To supply water to drive the dam's turbines, they also plan to build a huge reservoir by flooding 69,000 acres (27,900 ha) of land.

The billion-dollar scheme is very controversial. By 2003, 1.2 million people will have to move, and one of China's most beautiful areas will be lost beneath the giant reservoir.

The Growth of Tourism

The opening up of China has given rise to a new industry—tourism. In the days of

Mao Zedong, there were very few tourists. In 1996, however, more than seven million people came to China to visit its historic cities and extraordinary landscapes. Most of these tourists came from Japan and the United States. After a massive building program, 3,270 tourist hotels are now open throughout China, providing 486,000 guest rooms.

Beijing attracts many foreign and Chinese tourists who come to visit the Forbidden City or to go outside the capital to see the Great Wall. The Terracotta Warriors of Xi'an also attract many visitors. Some Buddhist monasteries and temples and other historic buildings in Tibet are now open to tourists. The government is spending a lot of money on restoring China's ancient buildings, many of which were neglected or even destroyed in the early years of communist rule.

TRANSPORTATION

The Chinese government has spent a lot of money on the national transportation system, but it is still not adequate. Geographical features such as mountains and deserts make access to some regions difficult, especially farther inland.

China has some 40 cities with a population of one million or more, but only four of these major cities—Beijing, Tianjin, Shanghai, and Guangzhou—have subway transportation to move crowds around. Although there are more car owners than before, most people still rely on buses, bicycles, motorbikes, and occasionally taxis to get around.

For long-distance travel, more people travel by train than by plane. The railroad system covers 39,776 miles (64,012 km), but it can carry only 60 percent of the country's freight. There is a high-speed train linking Nanjing and Shanghai, which travels at top speeds of 100 miles (160 km) per hour. Other high-speed links are planned on routes from Beijing to Harbin, Shanghai, and Guangzhou.

MAIN OVERSEAS ARRIVALS

%

27 Japan

13 United States

6 Russian Federation

5 United Kingdom

44 Others

Source: Government of China

The majority of visitors to China are overseas Chinese, many of whom come to see relatives. Many business people come from Japan, but there are also increasing numbers of tourists from the West.

Since 1988 the government no longer holds a monopoly on air travel. Many airlines now operate, including Air China, China Eastern, and Great Wall.

TRANSPORTATION

Since 1949 China has put in place a basic national road and rail network. Today all the provinces and regions, with the exception of Tibet, are connected by rail. Waterways, such as the Chang River and the Grand Canal, remain a crucial part of China's transportation system.

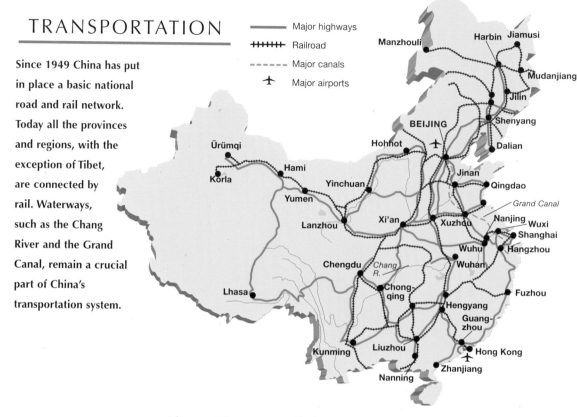

Major highways
Railroad
Major canals
Major airports

Manzhouli Harbin Jiamusi
Mudanjiang
Jilin
BEIJING Shenyang
Ürümqi Hohhot Dalian
Korla Hami
Yinchuan Jinan
Yumen Qingdao
Grand Canal
Lanzhou Xi'an Xuzhou Nanjing Wuxi
Shanghai
Wuhu Hangzhou
Chengdu Chang R. Wuhan
Lhasa Chong-qing Fuzhou
Hengyang
Guang-zhou
Kunming Liuzhou Hong Kong
Zhanjiang
Nanning

Almost 20 percent of China's villages are not connected to the main road network. By 2020, however, the government plans to build 18,645 miles (30,000 km) of super-highways linking China's main urban centers, such as Beijing and Shanghai. As China's people grow richer, the number of private automobiles on the road is increasing.

China's eight big ports operate at capacity, and still cannot handle all the ships. Some 50 percent of the ships have to wait days before they can be unloaded. Hong Kong has an excellent natural harbor and handles about 40 percent of China's exports.

The government is working to improve the inland waterways, once China's most important form of trans–portation. The Chang River is navigable for some 600 miles (950 km), and the Grand Canal is being gradually upgraded (see box opposite). Today water transportation accounts for about 33 percent of internal freight traffic.

There are more than 300 million bicycles in China, more than in any other country. Chinese must have a license to ride a bike.

The Grand Canal

In addition to its great natural rivers, China has more than 100,000 miles (160,900 km) of man-made waterways (*see* map opposite). One of the greatest engineering projects of all time is the Grand Canal, which was developed over almost 2,000 years. Work began on the canal in the early fifth century B.C. and was completed at the end of the 13th century A.D.

According to historians, more than a million people worked on the construction of the canal. The Grand Canal is the longest canal on Earth, although not all of it is currently navigable. Running north to south for more than 1,120 miles (1,800 km), the long waterway originally allowed easier transportation of rice and weapons between north and south.

Poor maintenance of parts of the Grand Canal caused it to become silted up by the end of the 19th century. In 1958 the government mobilized hundreds of thousands of people to work on three different sections of the canal, so that ships could travel along it again.

Today boats on the canal transport bulky goods such as coal and foodstuffs. The canal is also a useful local transportation link. In the photo below, farmers transport hay along the canal.

Arts and Living

"Simply by being a good son and friendly to his brothers, a man can exert an influence on government."

Confucius (551–479 B.C.), quoting from the ancient Chinese classic *Shu Ching*

The philosophy of the great Chinese thinker Confucius long taught the Chinese people to value the old ways of doing things and to respect authority. For centuries, as the various imperial dynasties came and went, people went on living much the same lives as their ancestors had done. Children respected the wishes of their parents; artists valued and imitated the work of the old masters; and in the temples people celebrated rites that had been practiced for hundreds of years.

The communist revolution of 1949 turned China upside down. The communist leaders wanted to transform China from a backward-looking country into a modern, forward-looking superpower. To do so, they decided to destroy China's past and to change completely the way people lived. Beautiful old buildings were torn down. Traditional art forms, such as the Beijing opera, were either banned or made to reflect the party's views. The lifestyles of ancient peoples such as the Mongolians and Tibetans were threatened with extinction.

Nevertheless, despite this attempt to wipe out the past, China's diverse cultures and lifestyles remain strong. The way today's Chinese people live together, eat and drink, worship, and make music continues to reflect China's age-old traditions. More recently the communist government, too, has begun to value the achievements of earlier times and works to preserve China's ancient buildings and arts.

Early in the morning, Chinese people gather in squares and parks to practice **taijiquan** *(tai chi), an ancient martial art, used today as a form of exercise.*

The Chinese value jade (a rare type of gemstone) very highly and believe it to have life-giving powers. There are many different colors of jade, from turquoise (blue-green) to black. The most prized is pure white.

This Ming porcelain bowl is decorated with a picture of playing children. The Mongols introduced this refined blue-and-white ceramic style in the early 14th century.

ARTS

The artistic traditions of China stretch back thousands of years. The tombs of China's earliest rulers very often contained objects made out of jade: carved tablets, swords, and simple flat disks. Over the centuries, the Chinese learned how to make and work with other materials such as bronze, paper, porcelain, and silk. Whatever the material, Chinese craftspeople worked with the same flair for careful detail and great refinement.

China has produced fine ceramics (including porcelain and pottery), paintings, poetry, and calligraphy (writing as an art form), as well as some remarkable buildings and beautiful gardens. Except for one or two names, Chinese artists and writers remain virtually unknown in the West. This is partly because of China's long isolation from the rest of the world but also because of the difficulties of translating Chinese into other languages.

From Pots to Porcelain

When Western people think of Chinese art, they may think of priceless Ming-dynasty (1368–1644) vases. These are made of beautifully shaped porcelain and decorated in blue and white depicting elements from the natural world such as pine, bamboo, or flowering plum. Objects such as these porcelain vases were often made for the emperor and his attendants at the Ming court.

The history of ceramics in China goes back much further than the Ming dynasty. The primitive Yangshao people, who lived about 8,000 years ago on the banks of the Huang River, painted pots with images of flowers, animals, and human faces. In the third century B.C., a whole army of baked terracotta (clay) lifesize soldiers was buried around the tomb of the first Qin emperor near Xi'an (*see* p. 54).

In the Yuan period (1279–1368), Chinese craftspeople invented the first true porcelain. They ground up a rock called petuntse into a fine powder and mixed this with a fine-textured, white clay called kaolin. They used the resulting paste to make vases, bowls, or figurines, which were fired at a high temperature (2,550°F or 1,400°C). The resulting material—porcelain—is hard, thin, and translucent (that is, light can pass through it). The name "porcelain" comes from the Italian word *porcellana*, meaning cowrie shell. The Venetian trader Marco Polo used the term to describe the astonishing new material he saw because it reminded him of the shell of the cowrie.

The secret of making porcelain stayed in the East until the early 18th century, when the first porcelain was successfully made in Europe, at Meissen in Germany, after years of experiments. Because it was so hard to obtain, porcelain became very highly prized in the West. It became so identified with the country where it originated that an alternative name for it was "china." The city of Jingdezhen, in China's southern Jiangxi province, was—and continues to be—an important center for producing porcelain in China.

During the Qing dynasty (A.D. 1644–1911), Chinese potters introduced more and more colors and more intricate designs into their products. This figurine of a laughing man was made in the late 17th or early 18th century.

Calligraphy: The Art of "Beautiful Writing"

Writing in China developed over thousands of years. It was originally used by monks and priests to keep records, but by the fourth century A.D., it had become a refined art form practiced by the aristocracy.

This highly refined kind of writing is called calligraphy, which means "beautiful writing." The Chinese thought that the way a person wrote revealed his or her personality and moral worth. During the Tang dynasty (A.D. 618–907), the calligrapher Tu Meng developed 120 different styles of writing, each of which emphasized a different aspect such as grace or skillfulness.

In the past the children of aristocrats and high court officials learned to write at an early age. Writing was considered not only a useful tool but also a social grace. A scholar could not pass the examination to become an imperial official unless he was a good calligrapher.

Chinese Writing

For a non-Chinese traveler in China who is trying to find the way through Beijing's busy streets or on the crowded subway, the intricate Chinese signs can look very confusing. This is because written Chinese is based not on letters but on "characters."

In some languages, such as English or French, words are written using an alphabet. This is a limited series of letters that represent different sounds. English uses a version of the Roman alphabet, with 26 letters. Chinese, by contrast, originally used pictographs ("picture-images"); that is, pictures of the thing or action they represented. Today each character represents either a word or a syllable.

Take the Chinese character for "east" (*dong*), for example:

It once represented a sun rising behind the branches and roots of a tree and meant "sunrise." Since the sun rises in the east, the character came to mean "east."

The Chinese word for "west" was originally a pictograph showing a bird returning to its nest when the sun sets.

Today it looks like this:

If the characters for "east" and "west" are written together (see below), they build a different word, meaning "thing:"

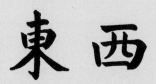

Many words are built out of two or more characters and many have more than one meaning, but written Chinese still needs a huge number of characters for all the words in the language. Instead of having to learn just 20 or 30 letters of an alphabet, Chinese people have to learn several thousand characters.

There are more than 50,000 characters in Chinese, although most of these are not used very often. To read a Chinese newspaper or a modern book, you need to know about 2,000 characters. Even a well-educated Chinese person is likely to know only about 6,000 characters.

Chinese character-writing has another important advantage. Because the characters are based on pictures rather than sounds, they are understood everywhere in China, even though the spoken word varies. For example, both

This girl learns some of the more simple Chinese characters in a school in Shanghai.

a person from Beijing and a person from Hong Kong understand the character

to mean "moon." Nevertheless, they pronounce this character differently. In Beijing people say "*yue,*" and in Hong Kong people say "*ut.*"

Even Chinese people find it very hard to learn how to read and write their language, and in the past the literacy rate was not high. In 1929 only 20 percent of people in China could read and write. This had risen to 80 percent by 1982. The Chinese communist government has attempted to make learning written Chinese much easier. It simplified the form of the 2,000 or so most common characters and introduced a system of writing Chinese using the Roman alphabet, called Pinyin (*see* p. 11). Pinyin is the form of Chinese used to write most of the names of people and places found in this book.

Before the invention of Pinyin, the most widely used system for writing Chinese characters in the Roman alphabet was the Wade-Giles system. It was developed in the 19th century, by British scholar Sir Thomas Francis Wade. Wade's system was modified in 1892 by Herbert A. Giles. The Pinyin and Wade-Giles systems produce very different results. For example, the Wade-Giles name for the Chinese capital is Peking, while the Pinyin name is Beijing.

You can see words spelled out in Pinyin in the big cities, on billboards, and on shop fronts. Generally Chinese people prefer the old, "difficult" characters, and the government has stopped its plan to make Pinyin the standard written Chinese.

The Chinese call the tools of the calligrapher—paper, brush, ink, and inkstone—the "four treasures of the scholar's study."

Calligraphers used, and still use today, paper (*see* p. 57), brushes made of animal hair, ink, and an inkstone. In the past, ink was dried into a solid block, so to make ink, a calligrapher broke off a piece of the block and rubbed it on an inkstone with some water.

The Art of the Brush Stroke

In the past, Chinese painters used brushes to paint with ink on paper or silk. Oil and canvas began to be used only in the 18th century under the influence of European painting. The paper and silk might be in the form of a handscroll (which unrolled horizontally), a hanging scroll (which unrolled vertically), a fan, or an album (which folded like a concertina). Influenced by calligraphy, much of the skill of painting lay in the quickness and control of the brushstrokes which the artist made.

Artists painted landscapes of mountains, bamboo, huts, lakes, and rivers; scenes from court life; and religious stories. Sometimes paintings included a poetic or philosophical inscription, which was meant to reflect the mood of the picture.

Handscrolls could be very long. One huge silk scroll shows Jiajing, a Ming emperor in the 16th century, in his state barge surrounded by the people of the court. The scroll measures more than 8 feet (2.5 m) and contains 915 figures.

The Chinese painter Lin-Tschun painted on silk this delicate image of a bird and ripening apples. Lin-Tschun worked during the Song dynasty (960–1279).

Silk and paper paintings were very fragile and were not intended for permanent display like a Western oil painting. People kept handscrolls and albums in waterproof camphorwood boxes until friends or art lovers visited. The paintings would then be unrolled or unfolded little by little on a table for the visitors to enjoy.

After the communists came to power, painters were obliged to glorify the revolution, and there was little room for free artistic expression. Artists produced gigantic statues of Mao or billboards showing crowds of workers smiling and waving the "Little Red Book." Since the late 1970s, there has been more artistic freedom. Today Beijing has a lively art scene, and many young Chinese artists exhibit their work in galleries overseas.

Poetry and Novels

The Chinese traditionally valued poetry and their poets very highly. From the Tang dynasty (A.D. 618–907) on, poetry formed part of the examination to become a civil-service (government) official. An educated man or woman was expected to be able to write poems, do calligraphy, and paint well. Emperors, too, often wrote poetry.

Silk

Silk, along with tea, is one of China's major contributions to the world. The material is woven from a thread produced by the silkworm moth. The caterpillar—called a silkworm— produces the thread to spin itself a cocoon. It takes about 13 pounds (6 kg) of cocoons to make slightly more than 2 pounds (1 kg) of raw silk. The finest-quality silk comes from silkworms that feed on the leaves of the mulberry tree. A coarser fiber is produced from the cocoons of other kinds of silkworm that feed on oak leaves.

The Chinese began to produce silk very early on. Evidence shows silk was first produced in 3000 B.C., when it was used for ceremonial garments. Silk was always a luxury good and symbolized wealth. The Chinese aristocracy and important court officials wore splendid robes of fine silk, such as the one above. Bolts (rolls) of silk cloth were sometimes used as payment.

The Silk Road, a trading route that linked China with Central Asia and Europe, was named after China's most successful export. Caravans of traders carried fine silk cloth as far as Rome, where an ounce (28 g) of silk was worth an ounce of gold. The Chinese kept the secret of making silk hidden until about the sixth century A.D.

This tradition continued into the 20th century. When the People's Liberation Army (PLA) took the city of Nanjing from the nationalists in April 1949, the communist leader Mao Zedong, wrote a poem to celebrate the triumph.

Traditional Chinese poetry often creates pictures of the real world. Chinese poets often described landscapes, the weather, the passing seasons, or animals and birds. They used these striking word-pictures to express their feelings. An 11th-century critic wrote: "Poetry presents the thing in order to convey the feeling. It should be precise about the thing and reticent [silent] about the feeling...this is how poetry moves us deeply."

Because Chinese is a very subtle language, it is often hard to translate the poetry into other languages. For this reason Chinese poetry is not very well known outside the country. Chinese novels, on the other hand, are much better known in the West.

One of the very greatest novels of imperial China is *The Dream of the Red Chamber* by Cao Xueqin. It was first published in 1792 and is about the fortunes of the wealthy Jia family, who live in the capital. The novel gives a remarkable insight into the daily life of an aristocratic household during the Qing dynasty: the elaborate dishes, such as bird's nest soup, served at mealtimes, the home remedies, the children's lessons, and the parties and festivals, as well as the many social rules.

One of China's best-known 20th-century writers is Lu Xun (1881–1936), who was also a poet. Lu Xun wrote about the need to modernize China through revolution. His short stories show how hard

A Chinese Poem

Du Mu (803–852) was a poet who wrote during the Tang dynasty. Like many Chinese poets, he was very sensitive to the beauties of the natural world. In this poem Tu Mu paints a picture of herons feeding in a river during spring. The poet does not express his own feelings directly in the poem, but the final lines are shot through with a gentle melancholy.

*Snowy coats and snowy crests
  and beaks of blue jade
Flock above the fish in the
  brook and dart at their own
  shadows,
In startled flight show up far
  back against the green hills.
The blossoms of a whole
  pear tree shed by the
  evening wind.*

The Book of Changes

According to legend, the great Chinese thinker Confucius (*see* p. 51) spent his last years editing five ancient books that he believed held the essence of traditional Chinese wisdom.

Collectively these are called the *Wu Jing*, or the *Five Classics of Confucianism*, and they have influenced Chinese writers for some 2,000 years.

The most popular of the *Five Classics* is *Yi Jing*, or *The Book of Changes*. The *Book of Changes* is a kind of fortune-telling manual, which is made up of 64 hexagrams (six-lined symbols) with an accompanying text. This hexagram (left) represents a new shoot struggling through the earth in the first days of spring. The six lines of a hexagram can be combined into different patterns. Each hexagram is based on two trigrams (sets of three of broken and unbroken lines).

The person who is looking for advice on what to do throws three coins or three sticks into the air. The pattern in which the coins or the sticks land is matched to a hexagram in the book and its corresponding meaning.

---

it was for the Chinese people to accept the changes that the new century brought. One of his best-known works is *The True Story of Ah Q* (1921).

"Healthy" and "Unhealthy" Music

Confucius believed that music could influence a person's mind and emotions and that it was an important part of education. Because of this, he also believed that the government should keep tight control over music. Bad music, he argued, could be "unhealthy."

Accordingly officials developed a formal kind of music for the imperial court and regulated musical matters just as they regulated weights and measures. Out in the countryside, however, there was a rich variety of folk musics that accompanied weddings, funerals, and temple fairs.

> "Therefore the ancient kings did not introduce... music merely to satisfy our senses but rather to teach people right taste and what is right and proper."
> 1st century B.C.
> Confucian writing.

The most important traditional Chinese instrument is the seven-stringed *qin*. The sound made by the *qin* is delicate and expressive, although today it is rarely learned or played outside music schools. Other traditional instruments are the pear-shaped, lutelike *pipa*, a three-stringed banjolike instrument called a *sanxian*, and the flute-like *xiao*.

In the early 20th century, traditional Chinese styles sometimes blended with European ones. The intoxicating "Cantonese music" popular in the 1920s was a kind of jazz in which Chinese instruments were played alongside saxophones and violins.

After Mao came to power in 1949, the communists frowned on traditional Chinese music as "unhealthy" and decadent because it was a reminder of past times. The Cultural Revolution effectively stopped all music except a small number of rousing marches and operas that were based on approved political themes.

This 18th-century painting shows musicians at the Qing court. Clockwise from top left, the women play the 16-string cheng, *the 4-string, lutelike* pipa, *the harplike* kong he, *the celesta-like* feng xiang, *and the* sheng, *a wind instrument.*

In the 1980s, however, Western-based popular music began to take hold in China. One of the first popular singers was Teresa Tang, whose sweet voice and melodies were a refreshing relief from years of political anthems and propaganda songs. Until the late 1980s, pop concerts were virtually unknown in China, and bands played at private parties and in front of small gatherings.

Chinese Opera

Music plays a central role in Chinese opera. This colorful and uplifting mix of song, dance, spoken dialogue, and acrobatics first developed more than 900 years ago. There were once more than 300 regional forms of opera, but the most famous was Beijing (Peking) Opera, which first developed during the 18th century. In the past troupes traveled from town to town, sometimes performing in the local teahouse, at New Year celebrations, or at a wedding or birthday party.

Traditional opera stories tell of unhappy lovers, ghosts, or famous warriors from Chinese history. The operas use no sets and very few props and in the past both male and female roles were played by male actors. Today actors and actresses wear elaborate, colorful costumes with flowing sleeves and fancy headdresses, and sing in high-pitched voices, accompanied by string instruments and percussion. It is said that this piercing style developed so that the actors could be heard over people talking in the audience.

Costumes and makeup are very stylized so that the audience knows instantly who the character is or how he or she will behave. For example, a face painted yellow and white represents cunning, while a red one means uprightness and loyalty. The gestures are also highly ritualized and can seem very puzzling to Westerners. Fingers running down a beard for instance, may indicate worry, while a leg lifted high may mean departure on horseback.

Under communist rule, the opera was reformed according to the ideas of Mao Zedong. During the Cultural

At the Movies

The Chinese government keeps a careful watch on the country's movie industry. This is because the government realizes that movies can be a powerful way of reaching millions of people with new ideas. Chinese people usually get to see a Chinese-produced fare of comedies and musicals, along with an occasional Hollywood blockbuster. *Titanic* (1998) was one of the most successful movies in China in recent years. The authorities allowed the movie to be shown because they said that the sinking of the *Titanic* was a symbol of how capitalism would collapse.

Some Chinese filmmakers such as Zhang Yimou have made movies that give a true-to-life picture of 20th-century China. Zhang's *To Live* (1992), for example, tells the story of an ordinary family as it struggles to survive three decades of communist rule. This film, along with many others, is banned in China.

Under British rule, Hong Kong was famous for its action movies. Actor Jackie Chan often uses his martial-arts skills in movie scenes that are both funny and action packed. After the Chinese takeover in 1997, it remained unclear to what extent the Chinese authorities would try to change the former colony's movie industry.

Feng Shui

Chinese buildings today are still planned according to the principles of feng shui that have been applied to architecture for thousands of years. Even modern skyscrapers in Hong Kong are built in this way. Feng shui is an ancient art based on Taoist ideas about the natural flow of energy, or *chi,* through the universe. Buildings have to be positioned so they do not disturb the spiritual balance of the surrounding landscape. They have to avoid unlucky points of the compass, such as the north, and use shapes and forms that are in harmony with the cosmos.

Revolution, it almost disappeared. Only a few new operas were composed, and they all celebrated the triumph of communism. Today, however, the Beijing opera has revived many of the traditional operas and performs new ones as well.

Palaces and Pagodas

Traditional Chinese buildings, whether temples, family homes, or emperor's palaces, usually take the same form: a walled compound (enclosed area) facing south to catch all the warmth of the winter sunshine and to avoid the "unlucky" north (*see* box). The entrance on the south side is hidden from passers-by by a screen and is sometimes guarded by a stone lion.

Buddhist, Confucian, and Taoist temples all have beautiful green or yellow roofs decorated with good-luck symbols such as carp and dragons. The buildings themselves are richly painted in red and gold, which for the Chinese mean joy and heaven.

Buddhist temples often also have a pagoda where sacred objects are stored. Pagodas are usually shaped like a very tall, thin triangle, and are several stories high. Each story has a roof that juts out a little over the story below. Worshipers go into the temples at any time, to pray, burn incense or paper, and give thanks.

During the Cultural Revolution, the communists destroyed thousands of China's old buildings. To house the workers for the new factories, many gray, concrete apartment houses were built. More recently, the government has tried to preserve and restore many of the surviving temples and other buildings.

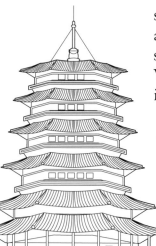

Pagodas—Buddhist temple towers—are found throughout the Far East. In China the pagoda is called a ta.

DAILY LIFE

Chinese life can be divided into two different lifestyles: rural life and city life. Although China has some very large cities, about 70 percent of people still live in rural areas. They work very hard and have few facilities compared to people living in cities. In urban areas the lifestyle is similar to that of any major city with shops, restaurants, and theaters, although living conditions are very crowded. China's cities attract young people from the countryside. It can be a struggle for the authorities to find jobs and accommodations for the millions of peasants who are seeking a better life in the city.

Town and Country

In many ways, life in the countryside has not changed very much in the last 50 years. Many areas have no electricity or running water. Labor-saving farm vehicles, such as tractors, are still too expensive for many farmers. Farmers in the countryside prefer to have a male

Old men sit playing cards in a teahouse. Many Chinese love to gamble and strongly believe in good and bad luck.

Modern Chinese
usually use the
metric system
of measurement.
Older people and
peasants, though,
sometimes
use traditional
measures.
These include:

chi = 3 feet
      (0.9 m)

li = 0.3 miles
      (0.5 km)

jin = 1.1 pounds
      (0.5 kg)

child in the family because boys are seen as long-term helpers on the farm. Traditionally girls leave their family when they get married and go to work with their husbands on the husband's family farm.

In China's cities most people live in apartments that have only two or three rooms. There is a severe housing shortage in China, so it is very common for parents to live with their children and grandchildren. Officially women retire from work at 55, while men end their working lives at 60, but the family will still expect them to work at home. It is very common, for example, for grandparents to care for a child while the parents are at work.

Pastimes and Pleasures

Because living conditions are so cramped, people have to conduct their leisure activities outside the apartment. In the mornings a popular form of exercise is *taijiquan* (*see* p. 92), known in the West as tai chi. It is a gentle,

Chinese Women

In traditional Chinese society, women were subordinate to men. In cities mothers bound the feet of young girls (aged 5 or 6) so that they were permanently deformed. Tiny "lily feet" were considered attractive and served to make women practically helpless outside the home. Women had to obey their father and, once married, their husband. A popular Chinese saying was: "A wife should be treated like a horse—driven and beaten regularly."

Some women became concubines— secondary wives who had to obey their husband and his chief wife. Older mothers could often be very powerful within the home and made the life of a son's wife a misery by scolding and beating her. Young wives often had to endure humiliating lives without rights.

Women's status improved after the communists came to power in 1949. The communists encouraged women to meet and discuss issues just as men did and to get jobs out of the home. Men and women today are officially equal, though in practice women still suffer some discrimination. For example, Chinese people are surprised if a woman has no male companion. Chinese women are also more likely to accept poorly paid work than Chinese men.

slow-motion fitness routine that can be practiced on any small piece of space available, but is usually performed in parks. *Taijiquan* is believed to help develop breathing, promote digestion, and improve muscle tone.

A popular activity for men who have retired is bird-keeping. In the mornings these men gather in parks with their bird, secure inside its bamboo cage, and compare their bird with others. Afterward the old men often gather in old-fashioned teahouses to drink tea and gossip.

Chinese cities now offer a great deal of fun for young people after decades of dullness. Since the early 1990s, discos and karaoke bars have become popular. In the bigger cities, nightclubs are common.

As the economy has changed, the choices for shoppers in China have become greater. In the past, cities usually had only one or two shops selling clothes. Luxury goods, such as sunglasses and radios, were very scarce. Today there are glittering department stores offering a range of high-quality Western and Chinese-made items. In the 1990s, multinational corporations opened hamburger and pizza restaurants in China. On its opening day in April 1992, more than 40,000 customers flocked to one American fast-food restaurant in central Beijing.

Improving Health Care

One of the most important changes brought by the communist revolution is the big improvement in the general level of public health. Health care is provided free or at low cost by the state, although as some prices have

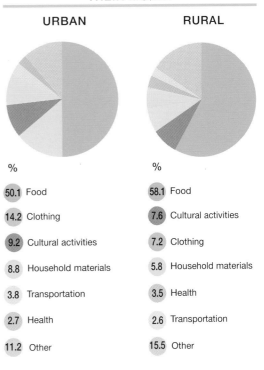

HOW THE CHINESE SPEND THEIR MONEY

URBAN

%

50.1 Food
14.2 Clothing
9.2 Cultural activities
8.8 Household materials
3.8 Transportation
2.7 Health
11.2 Other

RURAL

%

58.1 Food
7.6 Cultural activities
7.2 Clothing
5.8 Household materials
3.5 Health
2.6 Transportation
15.5 Other

Source: Government of China, 1993

The charts above show the comparative expenditures of rural and urban families.

On average Chinese men now live to age 68, and women to 71.

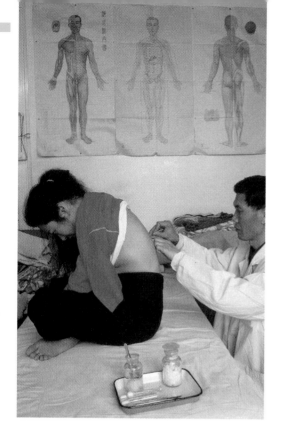

Acupuncture is a popular traditional Chinese remedy. A doctor inserts needles into various points on the patient's body. Each point corresponds to a specific organ; so, for example, the heart can be treated through the feet.

increased, people sometimes find that they do not have enough money to pay for the necessary medications.

Another problem is the gap between the standard of health care available in the major cities and in remoter, rural regions. While Beijing and Shanghai have excellent hospitals, with state-of-the-art medical equipment, places such as Tibet and Mongolia have only basic services.

In hospitals both Chinese and Western style medical care is available. Depending on what illness they have, many people prefer *zhongyi*, traditional Chinese methods of treating illnesses, to *xiyi*, which uses modern drugs or surgery. The use of herbs to cure ailments remains popular, as sometimes herbal medicines may have fewer side effects than modern drugs.

Modern research shows that some herbal treatments have a chemical basis that is similar to the chemical compounds used in modern medications. Nuts in Guangxi province have been dried and ground into powder to help treat rheumatism for more than 1,000 years. Research showed that this herbal treatment contains a large amount of a chemical compound that was used in the West for treating the same medical condition.

Education for All

Education in China is compulsory for young people between 6 and 16 years, and class sizes are often large. The school day runs from 7:45 A.M. until 4 P.M., five days a week. There are two terms, September to January and March to June. The beginning of the long summer holiday marks the end of the school year, while the Spring Festival holiday in February is the halfway point (*see* p. 112).

In elementary (primary) schools, Chinese children study reading, writing, mathematics, and history. Students begin junior middle (secondary) school at age 11 or 12. There they study more subjects, including literature, sciences, and foreign languages. At age 16, children move on to college or a technical school.

Students take exams at the end of elementary and junior school and college. In addition, students must pass an entrance examination to go on to higher (tertiary) education. Since Mao died, students are allowed to choose the subjects they want to study and are permitted to study at overseas universities.

Working Life

In state-run factories, employees work eight hours a day, six days a week. There are nine public holidays each year when workers take time off. Working hours are usually 8 A.M. to 5 P.M, with one hour for breaks.

The booming coastal regions have drawn many people from poorer regions, and there are factories that make employees work longer than the time set down by law. In areas such as Guangdong province, factories also provide living space for workers in the factory complex. These areas are often overcrowded and dirty.

ATTENDANCE AT SCHOOL

Tertiary	2%
Secondary	44%
Primary	100%

To improve educational standards, the Chinese government has set a target of nine years of schooling for all.

The Little Emperors

China, with 1.23 billion people, is home to nearly a quarter of the world's population. To reduce population growth, China has taken extreme measures, including the 1979 "One-Child Policy" that allows each couple to have only one child. Couples living in towns and cities who have a second child are punished with heavy fines. In Beijing a couple would face a fine of at least 10 percent of their annual income for having two children. In the countryside couples are sometimes allowed to have a second child. Some ethnic groups, such as Tibetans and Mongolians, or people living in Hong Kong, are not restricted either. The children of the "one-child" generation are often so spoiled by their parents and grandparents that they are called "little emperors."

How to Say...

Learning to speak Chinese is often very difficult for Westerners. In the first place, the everyday Chinese spoken in a city such as Shanghai is very different from the language spoken in Beijing. There are eight major dialects of Chinese, and each of these is so different from the others that a speaker of Shanghainese (or Wu in Chinese) is not able to understand a speaker of Cantonese (Yue).

To communicate with other provinces or with people from minorities who speak a different language, Chinese people speak Mandarin, which is the dialect of Chinese spoken in Beijing and the official language of the People's Republic. The Chinese call this standard language *putonghua*, which means "common speech." One good thing about the written characters is that everyone can understand what they mean, even if the word that the character represents sounds different in each dialect.

Speaking Chinese is also difficult because the tone of voice you use for a word is as important as the way you say it. Most dialects of Chinese have four different tones for each character, and each tone can give the word a different meaning. The high tone is very flat, almost robotlike, and is marked in Pinyin by a bar (¯) over the vowel. The rising tone, marked by an acute accent (´), is like the tone we use in English when we are offering alternatives—for example the tone of the word *black* in "Black or white?" The falling-rising tone is used in English when echoing someone's words with disbelief ("Mark's dead."—"De-ad?!") and is marked by a small v-like accent (ˇ). Finally, the falling tone, marked by a grave accent (`), is used in English, for example, when a lieutenant orders his soldiers to march in time—"Left! Right! Left! Right!"

Here are a few Mandarin words and phrases to try out. These are written using the Pinyin system and are followed by a guide to the pronunciation.

Hello/How are you? *Nǐ hǎo* (nee ow)
Goodbye *Zàijiàn* (dsi-jee-ahn)
Thank you *Xièxie* (shyeah-shyeah)
I'm sorry *Duìbùqǐ* (dway-bou-chee)
It doesn't matter *Méishì* (may-shee)
My name is… *Wǒ xìng* (wa shing)
There is no one word for "yes" or "no" in Chinese. To say "yes" the Chinese repeat the question in a short form. To say "no" they repeat the question, adding the negative word, *bú* (bou).

Numbers

One *Yī* (yee)
Two *Èr* (ur)
Three *Sān* (sahn)
Four *Sì* (see)
Five *Wǔ* (wou)
Six *Liù* (lee-ou)
Seven *Qī* (chee)
Eight *Bā* (bah)
Nine *Jiǔ* (jee-ou)
Ten *Shí* (shee)

Workers often work more than 12 hours a day on the factory floor. They put up with the conditions because many are young people from the countryside who can earn as much during a few months in the factory as they would in a year on the farm. They send a large part of their wages home to help their family. Others save money to set up small businesses when they return to their village.

Holidays and Festivals

The Chinese calendar year is rich in colorful festivals and traditional ceremonies. Many of them take place in or around China's Buddhist and Taoist temples. The festivals follow the traditional Chinese lunar (moon) calendar (*see* box).

The most important holiday in China is Spring Festival, which marks the beginning of spring. This is also known as the Chinese New Year. The Spring Festival starts on the first day of the first month of the lunar calendar. This usually falls in late January or early February. In the year 2000, for example, the Spring Festival began on February 5. Spring Festival has many traditions and rituals. It includes spring cleaning homes to sweep away traces of bad luck from the old year. People get a haircut and pay off all debts as a symbolic new start to life.

The eve of Spring Festival is a strictly family occasion with set traditions. Dinner is often a feast of seafood, and people often wear red as this color is believed to keep away evil spirits. The rest of the

> In China each year is associated with an animal from a cycle of 12. Which is your birth sign?
>
> **1990 Horse**
> **1991 Goat**
> **1992 Monkey**
> **1993 Rooster**
> **1994 Dog**
> **1995 Pig**
> **1996 Rat**
> **1997 Ox/Cow**
> **1998 Tiger**
> **1999 Rabbit**
> **2000 Dragon**
> **2001 Snake**

The Lunar Calendar

The traditional Chinese calendar is very different from the Western calendar because it follows the phases of the moon rather than the sun. The 336-day lunar year has 12 lunar months of 28 days. It is shorter than the 365-day solar year, so every few years, an extra month has to be added to make up the difference. Traditionally poets and painters celebrated the beauty of the moon, and it still holds a special place in Chinese life.

Today the Chinese government has adopted the Western solar year, but the lunar calendar remains very important. The dates of festivals, including Spring Festival, depend on the lunar year, and many people working on the land plant and harvest their crops according to the traditional calendar.

meal might have steamed dumplings or a dessert made with sweetened sticky rice. As midnight approaches, families set off firecrackers to drive away evil spirits.

The Spring Festival for the Chinese is like Christmas for Westerners. It is a time of forgetting grudges, of thinking of peace and happiness, of family unity, and of good food. Instead of Merry Christmas, Chinese wish each other "Guo Nian," meaning "passing the year."

The Mid-Autumn (Fall) Festival is sometimes called the Moon Festival. This takes place on the 15th day of the eighth moon of the lunar year. To celebrate this day, people admire the full moon, eat delicious moon cakes, and set off noisy, colorful fireworks.

New Year celebrations end with the Lantern Festival, when people march through the street waving multi-colored paper lanterns and making music. The festival dates back to the Han dynasty (206 B.C.–A.D. 220).

Another important festival is Qing Ming, which is known as the Sweeping of the Graves. During Qing Ming families visit the graves of family members and sweep the tomb stones, replant flowers around the tomb, and burn incense or money.

Traditionally such festivals were also public holidays. Under the Cultural Revolution only Spring Festival remained as a public holiday. Today there are nine national holidays.

Fireworks

Chinese New Year celebrations would not be complete without the deafening crackle of thousands of firecrackers. Firecrackers date back to the third century A.D. when they were simply bamboo pieces thrown into a fire that exploded when the heat reached the air trapped in the stalk.

The firecracker was transformed in the tenth century when Chinese chemists invented gunpowder—an explosive mixture of saltpeter, sulfur, and charcoal. At first the Chinese used this dangerous substance to make weapons, developing primitive forms of the gun and grenade.

But the Chinese also used gunpowder to make fireworks, which they used to create dazzling displays during festivals. Soon they had created an entire arsenal of spectacular fireworks, from powerful rockets to so-called water rats, which were fireworks that sped across water spewing flames behind them. By adding different chemicals to the basic gunpowder mixture, the Chinese discovered that they could create an astonishing range of colors and sounds.

A stunning firework display (*above*) accompanied the celebrations that marked the return of Hong Kong to China in 1997.

A World-class Cuisine

Chinese food is famous around the world for being one of the great cuisines. The Chinese consider cooking to be a subtle and delicate art. For outsiders the first noticeable difference is that the various foods placed on the table are for people to share. The Chinese use chopsticks instead of a knife and fork and many wipe their hands on a napkin resting on their stomach after eating.

For a Westerner many Chinese dishes can seem unusual. In some parts of China, it is still common to eat such dishes as dog stew or shark's fin soup. In the southern province of Guangdong, there is a local saying that says the Cantonese "eat anything with four legs except the dinner table."

Chinese food has distinct local flavors, and there are many regional variations in cooking styles. In the West, one of the most familiar kinds of Chinese food is Cantonese, which has its origins in the southern city of Guangzhou. Cantonese food is famous for its delicate flavors. The food is often steamed instead of fried and, because of the favorable climate and rich soil, fresh vegetables are included in most dishes. The most famous Cantonese meal is *dim*

Oodles of Noodles

The Chinese are very fond of noodles. In China, noodles, or *mianto*, usually come in the form of slippery, threadlike strips and are often made from rice rather than wheat flour. According to legend Marco Polo (*see* p. 62) brought noodles back to Italy after his visit to China. In Italy, as pasta, they became a staple of the Italian diet. Here is a simple Chinese recipe for noodles with a soy-sauce dressing.

Serves four people

½ lb (225 g) fresh Chinese noodles

2 tbs sesame oil

3 tbs soy sauce

1 tbs white vinegar

1 crushed garlic clove

½ tsp of sugar

4 oz (115 g) fresh mung-bean sprouts,
   washed and drained

4 crisp lettuce leaves, shredded

Bring two quarts (2 l) of water to a boil in a large pan. (Ask an adult to help you with this, as boiling water can be dangerous.) Drop in the noodles and allow the water to come to the boil again. Add 8 fluid ounces (¼ l) of cold water and bring to a boil again. Pour in another 8 fluid ounces (¼ l) of cold water and let the water come to a boil for a third time. Drain the noodles in a colander and then run cold water over them. Finally place them in a serving bowl. Combine the sesame oil, soy sauce, vinegar, garlic, and sugar in a bowl. Add the sprouts and shredded lettuce to the noodles, pour in the dressing and toss.

sum, which literally means "touch the heart." *Dim sum* consists of a variety of delicacies and is usually served for breakfast or dinner. In restaurants the food is brought on carts and includes succulent roast-pork buns and prawn-filled dumplings.

Chinese banquets are extremely formal occasions and follow a strict set of rules. For example, according to custom, the host should always sit opposite the entrance, ready to greet his or her guests. Guests often greet new arrivals to a banquet with applause, and the newcomer also applauds. It is considered very rude to arrive late. Banquets are often very lavish and can easily include ten different courses. The Chinese think it is far better to serve up too much food rather than too little. Leaving your bowl empty implies that your host has been miserly.

A family enjoys a meal on a barge on the Grand Canal. The Chinese traditionally eat from shared bowls rather than from separate plates. Each person at a meal holds a bowl in which he or she places selected foods from the common bowls.

Traditional Beliefs Today

China is officially an atheist nation. Under Mao, many places of worship in China were closed. The Red Guards destroyed many Buddhist temples and monasteries, and monks were sometimes killed or forced to work in the countryside. Since Mao's death, however, the government has allowed some Buddhist and Taoist temples to reopen and tolerates some religious worship.

In 1974, toward the end of the Cultural Revolution, the communists launched a campaign against Confucianism. Today, however, Confucianist values, such as respect for authority, are once again fashionable in China. The government still frowns on Christianity. Christianity was banned under Mao. Christian churches are strictly controlled today and Western missionaries are banned from entering the country. Nevertheless, in the 1980s and 1990s, Christianity gained in popularity and new churches are being built.

In July 1999 the government banned a religious sect called Falun Gong. It declared the sect an "anti-government political force" and ordered police to detain around 5,000 of its members.

The Future

"The empire, long united, must divide; long divided, must unite. Thus it has always been."

The Romance of Three Kingdoms, a classic Chinese novel

It is difficult to be indifferent to what happens to China. Its vast size, huge population, economic power, and military strength mean that the country is ready to play a key role not just in the future of Asia but of the whole world. How well this great nation succeeds in the next few decades is something that many people are concerned about.

Some Western experts give dire warnings about the dangers of a future superpower China. Others talk about the imminent collapse of this ancient giant. The Chinese themselves like to quote the above lines from classic literature. Throughout its history, they say, China has united, then collapsed, only to be reunited again. Why should it be any different now? What is clear is that China today stands at another crucial moment in its development.

ON THE RAILROAD TRACK

When Chinese people talk about their country's future, they often mention the idea of *jie gui*. This literally means "railroad track," but refers to China's determination to compete economically with the rest of the world.

China has a long, uphill struggle ahead if it is to meet this goal. On the positive side, China has an enormous wealth of natural resources. There are vast reserves of coal and large oil fields, as well as an abundance of other mineral resources. China's powerful rivers mean that

FACT FILE

● The Chinese government has set itself an ambitious goal for economic growth. It hopes to double the country's gross national product (GNP) between the years 2000 and 2010.

● China will continue to face demands from its peoples for greater self-rule and more freedom of rights. China's relationship with Tibet remains an issue of international concern.

● The Tenth Five-Year Plan (2000–2004) keeps strict controls over the economy, while encouraging free-market competition among private businesses.

Chinese schoolchildren studying in a classroom. As the Chinese people become richer and better educated, will they demand more political rights?

there is great opportunity for hydroelectric power. The return of Hong Kong to China has provided it with a powerful injection of capital and business know-how. There is also a huge workforce in China, eager to improve the country's standard of living.

On the negative side, there are important problems that China has to tackle in order to build a successful economy. The size of China's population will remain a key issue for decades to come. The rate of growth is expanding even today, and with ever-increasing life expectancy, the population is getting older. The problem is that the production of food may be outstripped by the numbers of mouths to feed, and there is a real possibility of famines again in the future.

China's rapid industrialization threatens the environment. One example is

Many Chinese cities are overcrowded. This high-rise apartment house is in Hong Kong, where the population density is some 15,500 people per square mile (6,000 per sq. km).

that soil from bare, deforested hillsides is being washed into China's rivers, where it builds up as silt on riverbeds and behind dams. The work of the river-control projects of the late 20th century is being undone, and Chinese people living in the countryside once again live in fear of devastating floods.

Can Communism and Capitalism Live Together?

The most important problem facing China, though, is a political one. At the moment the Chinese system is an unusual combination of capitalism and communism. The main difficulty is how the Communist Party can continue to set five-year economic plans, with production targets and quotas, for a Chinese market that today operates in part on a freer movement of supply and demand for goods and services. It is possible that powerful business people may begin to demand more control in the future.

Moreover, if the experiment with capitalism goes wrong, there could be a strong reaction from "hardline" (traditional) communists. These hardliners could insist on a return to communist values and an end to the free market economy. This could result in foreign investors taking their money out of the country. China's hard-won changes would be lost.

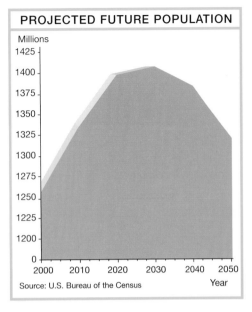

PROJECTED FUTURE POPULATION

Millions

Source: U.S. Bureau of the Census

Year

Old and Young

Today's young people have very different ideals and expectations from those of their parents, who experienced the 1949 revolution. They are often better educated than the last generation and have traveled and sometimes studied overseas. There is more money in people's pockets, and their homes now have refrigerators, televisions, and stereos, something unimaginable to them just a short time ago.

Improvement in China's standard of living may divert attention from political demands. Nevertheless, there is growing dissatisfaction with China's system of government. As the old leadership dies, a new generation of leaders may be more willing to accept political change. There are already some promising signs. For example, in the 1990s one reform allowed villages with a population of under 10,000 to elect their own leaders. Optimists argue that this is just the beginning of a trend toward Western-style democracy throughout China.

Whatever happens to China in the 21st century, its people will be sure to endure. Throughout their country's long history, they have survived famines, wars, revolutions, and other upheavals and still kept their national identity and their rich culture very much alive.

Experts predict that China's population will peak in about 2030 and then decrease rapidly. This future decline in population size will depend on the continuation of the one-child policy and China's economic prosperity.

Almanac

POLITICAL

Country name:
Official form: People's Republic
of China
Short form: China
Local official form: *Zhonghua Renmin
Gongheguo*
Local short form: *Zhong Guo*

Nationality:
Noun: Chinese
Adjective: Chinese

Official language: Mandarin

Capital city: Beijing

Type of government: communist state

Suffrage (voting rights): 18 years and
over; universal

Overseas territories: none

National anthem: "Arise you who
refuse to be slaves"

National day: October 1

Flag:

GEOGRAPHICAL

Location: eastern Asia; latitudes
20° to 53° north and
longitudes 74° to 135° east.

Climate: The north and west
are semi-arid or arid,
with extreme temperature
variations. The south and
southeast are warmer and
more humid.

Total area: 3,691,500 square miles
(9,560,900 sq. km)
land: 97.2%
water: 2.8%

Coastline: 8,700 miles (14,000 km)

Terrain: Mostly mountainous, high
plateaus, deserts in west; plains,
deltas, and hills in east.

Highest point: Mount Everest,
29,028 feet (8,848 m)
Lowest point: Turpan Depression,
505.2 feet (-154 m)

Natural resources: zinc, petroleum,
lead, coal, iron ore, mercury, tin,
tungsten, antimony, manganese,
molybdenum, vanadium,

magnetite, aluminum, uranium, hydroelectric power potential

Land use (1993 est.):
arable land: 10%
forests and woodland: 14%
permanent pasture: 31%
other: 45%

Natural hazards: tsunamis, volcanoes, earthquakes, typhoons, flooding, and droughts

POPULATION

Population (1998 est.): 1.237 billion

Population growth rate (1998 est.): 0.83%

Birth rate (1998 est.): 15.73 births per 1,000 of the population

Death rate (1998 est.): 6.99 deaths per 1,000 of the population

Sex ratio (1996 est.): 106 males per 100 females

Total fertility rate (1998 est.): 180 children born for every 1,000 women in the population

Infant mortality rate (1998 est.): 45.46 deaths per 1,000 live births

Life expectancy at birth (1998 est.):
total population: 69.59 years
male: 68 years female: 71 years

Literacy (1995 est.):
total population: 81.5%
male: 89.9% female: 72.7%

ECONOMY

Currency: yuan (¥); 1¥ = 10 jiao
Exchange rate: $1 = 8.3¥

Gross national product (GNP) (1997): $906 billion (seventh-largest economy in the world)

Average annual growth rate (1990–1996): 12.3%

GNP per capita (1996 est.): $750

Average annual inflation rate (1990–1997): 10.9%

Unemployment rate (1997): 4%

Exports (1996): $151.2 billion
Imports (1996): $138.9 billion

Aid received (1993): $1.977 billion

Human Development Index
(an index scaled from 0 to 100 combining statistics indicating adult literacy, years of schooling, life expectancy, and income levels within a country):
62.6 (U.S. 94.2)

TIME LINE—CHINA

World History   **Chinese History**

c. 600,000 B.C.

***c.* 40,000** Modern humans—*Homo sapiens sapiens*—emerge.

***c.* 600,000** *Homo erectus* living in China.

***c.* 8000** Beginnings of agriculture.

c. 3000 B.C.

1379 Akhenaten is king of Egypt.

***c.* 1100** Phoenicians develop first alphabetic script.

***c.* 1600** Shang dynasty founded.

1027 Zhou dynasty founded.

c. 750 B.C.

612 Fall of Assyrian empire.

***c.* 563** Birth of Siddhartha Gautama, the Buddha.

327 Alexander the Great invades India.

***c.* 650** Chinese begin to cast iron.

551 Birth of Confucius.

221 Qin Shihuangdi becomes the first emperor of China.

214 Great Wall of China completed.

206 Han dynasty founded.

1620 Pilgrims land in New England.

1492 Columbus lands in America.

1453 Constantinople falls to the Turks.

1445 Gutenberg prints the first European book.

1095–1099 The First Crusade.

800 Charlemagne, king of the Franks, becomes first Holy Roman Emperor.

476 Goths sack Rome.

98–117 Roman empire reaches its greatest extent.

***c.* 30** Crucifixion of Jesus.

c. A.D. 0

1644 The Manchus conquer China; beginning of the Qing dynasty.

1514 Portuguese ships reach China.

1403–1433 Chinese voyages to India and Africa.

1368 Ming dynasty founded.

c. 1300

1279 Kublai Khan completes conquest of China.

960 Song dynasty founded.

868 Earliest surviving printed book produced.

641 A Chinese princess marries the king of Tibet.

618 Tang dynasty founded.

589 Sui dynasty reunites China.

***c.* 65** Buddhism reaches China.

c. 1700

1775–1783 American War of Independence.

1789 Revolution breaks out in France.

1815 Napoleon is defeated at Waterloo.

1861–1865 American Civil War.

1720 Tibet becomes part of Qing empire.

1839–1842 First Opium War.

1842 Hong Kong Island given to Britain.

1851–1864 Tai Ping rebellion.

1858–1860 Second Opium War.

2000 The West celebrates the Millennium.

1999 The Kosovo conflict in Europe.

1999 Portugal hands back port of Macau to China.

c. 2000

c. 1900

1914–1918 World War I.

1917 Revolution brings communism to Russia.

1933 Adolf Hitler becomes German chancellor.

1936–1939 Spanish Civil War.

1939–1945 World War II.

1898–1900 The Boxer uprising.

1911 End of imperial China: foundation of the Republic of China.

1921 First meeting of the Chinese Communist Party.

1934 The Long March begins.

1949 Foundation of the People's Republic of China.

1994 End of apartheid in South Africa.

1992 Democrat Bill Clinton becomes U.S. president.

1991 Break up of the Soviet Union.

1989 Communism collapses in Eastern Europe; fall of the Berlin Wall.

1998 President Clinton visits China.

1997 Britain hands back Hong Kong to China.

1997 Deng Xiaoping dies.

1989 Tiananmen Square massacre.

1976 Death of Mao Zedong.

c. 1975

1965 Start of U.S. involvement in Vietnam War.

1961 Berlin Wall erected.

1953 Death of Stalin.

1950 Beginning of the Korean War.

1972 President Nixon visits China.

1966 Beginning of the Cultural Revolution.

1958 The Great Leap Forward.

1951 The Chinese army takes control of Tibet.

c. 1950

Glossary

autonomous region: A self-governing area within a larger nation.

Buddhism: A religion of eastern and Central Asia based on the teachings of the prophet Siddartha Gautama (the Buddha). Buddhism preaches self-denial as a means of salvation.

calligraphy ("beautiful writing"): Elegant handwriting.
communism: A political system in which goods and land are owned by everyone and there is no private property.
Confucianism: A system of beliefs based on the writings of the Chinese philosopher Confucius (551–479 B.C.). Confucianism emphasizes the importance of obedience, both within the family and society.
consumer goods: Manufactured goods ready for sale directly to the public—for example, cars and clothes.
Cultural Revolution: Chairman Mao's attempt to reorganize Chinese society on communist lines, between 1966 and 1970.

dialect: A regional variation of a national language.
dowager: A widow who inherits her husband's position or property.
dynasty: A succession of rulers who all belong to the same family.

exports: Goods sold by one country to another.

foreign debt: The amount of money owed by a nation to the rest of the world.
free enterprise: A system by which private businesses can operate without intervention from government.

Grand Canal: A canal that runs for more than 1,120 miles (1,800 km) between northern and southern China.
Great Wall: A wall 3,750 miles (6,035 km) long constructed over several centuries to keep northern invaders out of China.
gross national product (GNP): The total value of goods and services produced by the people of a country during a period, usually a year.

hydroelectricity: Electricity produced by harnessing the water power in a river.

imports: The goods bought by one country from another.
inflation: The annual rate at which prices increase in a country.

karst: A limestone landscape featuring rock formations that have been eroded into unusual shapes and caverns.
kowtow: To kneel and touch one's forehead to the floor out of respect for someone.

Kuomintang (KMT): The Chinese nationalist party.

Long March: A 6,000-mile (9,600 km) trek made by communists under Mao Zedong in 1934 to avoid the KMT.

Manchus: A people from Manchuria who conquered China in 1644 and set up their own dynasty, the Qing.
municipality: A self-governing city usually administered by a central government.

National People's Congress (NPC): China's parliament, responsible for approving policy decisions made by the Politburo.

pagoda: A towerlike structure in a Buddhist temple; used to store sacred objects.
peninsula: A finger of land that stretches out into the sea.
People's Liberation Army (PLA): China's national army—one of the most powerful armies in the world.
Pinyin: A system of representing Chinese words using letters of the Roman alphabet rather than Chinese symbols or characters.
Politburo: A committee of CCP (Chinese Communist Party) members that represents the highest authority in China's government.

radicalism: A political philosophy that promotes extreme change in society.
Red Guards: Militant communist university and high-school students who banded together in 1966. Their devotion to Chairman Mao led them to violent acts against any whom they felt to be anticommunist.
reincarnation: The rebirth of life-forms, especially the rebirth of a soul in a new body. Reincarnation is

an important part of Buddhist belief.

silt: A deposit of material or sediment, often carried by a river.
Special Economic Zone (SEZ): Coastal regions in China that have been allowed special business conditions, such as lower rates of tax, to encourage foreign investment.
steppe: A vast, treeless plain found in southern Russia and Central Asia.

Taoism: Chinese system of beliefs that advises people on how to act in harmony with nature in order to live a long and prosperous life.
Tiananmen Square Massacre: The killing of an unknown number of pro-democracy protesters and students by the PLA in Beijing's Tiananmen Square on June 4, 1989.
tundra: Treeless plains of subarctic regions. The soil below surface level is usually permanently frozen.

Bibliography

Major Sources Used for This Book
Bonavia, D. *The Chinese: A Portrait*. Harmondsworth: Penguin, 1981.
Ebrey, P. *Cambridge Illustrated History of China*. Cambridge: CUP, 1996.
Haw, S. *Traveller's History of China*. Moreton: Windrush Press, 1995.
Spence, J. *The Gate of Heavenly Peace*. Harmondsworth: Penguin, 1983.

General Further Reading
Cootes, R.J., and L.E. Snellgrove. *The Ancient World*. New York: Longman, 1991.
The DK Geography of the World. New York: Dorling Kindersley, 1996.
The Kingfisher History Encyclopedia. New York, NY: Kingfisher, 1999.
Lunine, J.I., and C.J. Lunine. *Earth: Evolution of a Habitable World*, New York: Cambridge University Press, 1999.
MacMillan, B., and G. Fell. *Atlas of Economic Issues*. New York: Facts on File, 1992.

Student Atlas. New York: Dorling Kindersley, 1998.
Taborelli, G. *Art: A World History*. New York: Dorling Kindersley, 1998.

Further Reading About China
Barnes, I., and others. *The History Atlas of Asia*. Foster City, CA: IDG Books Worldwide, 1998.
Hoobler, T., and others. *Confucianism*. New York: Facts on File, 1993.
Liu Sanders, T.T. *Dragons, Gods, and Spirits from Chinese Mythology (World Mythology Series)*. New York: Peter Bedrick Books, 1994.
Sis, P. *Tibet: Through the Red Box*. New York: Farrar, Straus, & Giroux, 1998.

Some Websites About China
www.abcnews.go.com/reference/countries
www.kidport.com/World Geography/ China/China.htm
www.surfnetkids.com/china.htm
hyperion.advanced.org/20443/land.html

Index

Acknowledgments

Cover Photo Credits
Tony Stone: Margaret Gowan (background); ET Archive: Victoria and Albert Museum (porcelain bowl); **Mary Evans Picture Library** (image of Confucius)

Photo Credits
AKG London: 57, 61, 66, 98, 99, 102; AP 77; Erich Lessing 50; Jürgen Sorges 56; **Duncan Brown:** 19; **Bruce Coleman:** Pacific Stock 35; **Corbis:** Derek Allan 113, Dean Conger 28; Eric Crichton 34; Stephanie Maze 116; Wally McNamee 92; Tom Nebbia 112; David Samuel Robbins 25; Joseph Sohm: ChromoSohn Inc 79; The Purcell Team 46; Peter Turnley 108; Julia Waterlow: Eye Ubiquitous 88; Michael S. Yamashita 87; **ET Archive:** 68;

Bibliotheque National Paris 53; British Library 58; Victoria and Albert Museum 94, 95; **Mary Evans Picture Library:** 51, 62, 64, 74; **Hutchison Library:** C. Dodwell 15; **Tony Stone Images:** Glen Allison 14; Bushnell / Soifer 43br; Julian Calder 54; Paul Chesley 118; D.E. Cox 43t, 97; Alain Le Garsmeur 91; Margaret Gowan 21; Yann Layma 22, 36, 39, 72, 80, 105, 115; Mike McQueen 41; Briggite Merle 33; Michel Setboun 26, 27; Vince Streano 6; Keren Su 12, 16, 31, 82; Tom Till 45; Art Wolfe 24.

Text Credit
The Publishers would like to thank Anchor Books/Doubleday for permission to reprint the quotation on p. 75 from Jung Chang, *Wild Swans: Three Daughters of China*.